This third book in the Master Thinking Skills series is designed to help children continue sharpening their critical thinking and reasoning skills. Exercises such as following directions and learning dictionary skills let them build on past work. They will study antonyms, homonyms and synonyms as well as gain skills in tracking and use of maps. Verbal analogies and verbal sequences are introduced in this book, and classifying and making deductions continue to add to their critical thinking skills. Also in Level 3 children will practice making inferences and they will be introduced to library skills.

Following Directions...3, 4, 5
Learning Dictionary Skills 6, 7, 8, 9
Review...10
Antonyms..11, 12
Homonyms..13, 14
Synonyms...15, 16, 17
Review...18
Tracking...19, 20, 21
Learning Map Skills...22, 23, 24, 25
Review...26
Verbal Analogies...27, 28, 29, 30
Verbal Sequencing 31, 32, 33
Review...34
Classifying 35, 36, 37
Making Deductions 38, 39, 40, 41
Review...42
Making Inferences 43, 44, 45, 46, 47, 48, 49
Review...50
Introducing Library Skills..51, 52, 53, 54, 55, 56, 57
Review...58
Finding the Main Idea 59
Recognizing Details 60
Finding the Main Idea 61, 62
Recognizing Details 63
Review...64
Enrichment Preview...65-72

Skills Glossary

Classifying. Putting things that are alike into categories.

Finding analogies. Comparing similarities.

Finding antonyms. Finding opposites.

Finding homonyms. Finding words that are spelled the same but sound different.

Finding synonyms. Finding words that are spelled different but have the same meaning.

Finding the main idea. Finding the most important points.

Following directions. Doing what directions say to do.

Inference. Using logic to figure out what is unspoken but evident.

Introducing library skills. Learning how to use the library.

Learning dictionary skills. Looking up words in the dictionary.

Learning map skills. Learning how to use a map.

Making deductions. To derive a conclusion by reasoning.

Recognizing details. Being able to pick out and remember the who, what, when, where, why and how of what is read.

Sequencing. Putting things in order.

Tracking. Following a path.

Name: _____

What A Nice Picture!

Directions: Curious Kate is looking for kings and queens. Put a check in the box after you have found what is listed.

☐ Artist	☐ Clock	☐ Barn
☐ Helicopter	☐ Sail boat	☐ Gate
☐ Duck	☐ Umbrella	☐ Mountains
☐ Horse	☐ Fence	☐ Lake
☐ Cart	☐ Sunflowers	☐ Cattails
☐ Bear	☐ Dog	☐ King

Name: _____

Curious Kate

Directions: Curious Kate continues looking for clues. She has found a secret message. Look at the code. Figure out what the message says.

1 = a
2 = b
3 = c
4 = d
5 = e
6 = f
7 = g
8 = h
9 = i
10 = j
11 = k
12 = l
13 = m
14 = n

15 = o
16 = p
17 = q
18 = r
19 = s
20 = t
21 = u
22 = v
23 = w
24 = x
25 = y
26 = z

20 8 5   19 1 22 9 14 7   17 21 5 5 14

_____

_____

23 1 19   19 20 21 14 7   2 25   1   2 5 5.

_____

_____

4

Name: _____

A Day At The Fair

Directions: Ann and Bill are at the fair. Read the story. Underline the 6 sentences in which Ann and/or Bill are happy.

Ann and Bill each have $5 to spend at the fair. As they walk to the fair, Ann thinks that she lost her money. She checks her pockets. Then she and Bill start looking in the grass. Finally Ann checks the pocket on her dress again and finds her money.
When Ann and Bill get to the fair they look at all the rides.
They decide to go on a roller coaster. They are quiet while they wait.
They scream when they are riding the roller coaster. When the ride is done, they get off laughing. Bill is hungry. Ann says, "Let's buy ice cream cones." As they eat their ice cream they play a few games.
Ann wins a big stuffed animal. Bill does not win anything. After three hours at the fair Ann and Bill are tired. As they walk home they talk about their exciting day.

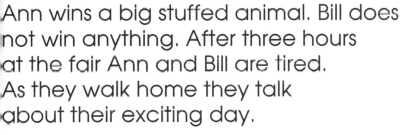

Looking Up Words In The Dictionary

Directions: Help Mrs. Posey find the names of her flowers in the dictionary.

Guide words are the first and last words on a dictionary page. All words on that page come between those two.

Look at the flower on the left. Circle the pair of guide words that the flower's name would be between.

1. rose   rain — refuse
                 rock — rode
                 (roar — ruler)

4. sunflower   slip — space
                  some — sun
                  such — swim

2. daisy   bait — bar
             dad — deck
             dare — delight

5. violet   vase — vent
              vine — visit
              visit — voice

3. tulip   tube — tug
            track — twin
            two — us

6. lily   lamb — late
            light — like
            light — line

Name: _____

Learning Dictionary Skills

Directions: Mrs. Posey is ready to plant. Unscramble these gardening words. Then circle the 10 words that come between **flower** and **glove** in the dictionary. The first one is done for you.

1. lyf   _____**fly**_____   9. rgass   _____

2. ridt   _____   10. grfo   _____

3. oodf   _____   11. reptty   _____

4. eeds   _____   12. lufl   _____

5. truif   _____   13. nedrag   _____

6. estfor   _____   14. ateg   _____

7. shvelo   _____   15. krae   _____

8. therga   _____   16. figt   _____

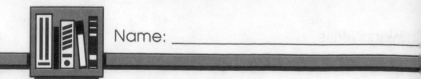

Dictionary Entries

Directions: Words in a dictionary are called entries. Some entries have more than one meaning. Dictionaries number each meaning. Look at the word and its meanings. Then answer the questions.

Fan — 1. An instrument shaped in a half-circle and waved by hand. 2. An instrument with rotating blades that stirs the air. 3. To cause air to blow. 4. A person with a special interest.

1. How many meanings are listed for **fan**? _____

2. Write the meaning listed that describes a baseball **fan**.

_____

_____

_____

3. What is the first meaning of **fan** listed?

_____

_____

_____

4. Read this sentence: She will **fan** herself because she is hot. What is the best meaning for **fan** as it is used in this sentence?

_____

_____

_____

5. Read the second meaning of **fan**. Now write a sentence using that kind of a **fan** in it.

_____

_____

_____

Name: _____

Using The Dictionary

Directions: Look up each word in a dictionary. Then write a sentence using it.

There are different kinds of dictionaries. Some are especially for children. Three of those are: *The American Heritage Children's Dictionary, Simon and Schuster's Illustrated Young Readers' Dictionary, and Macmillan Dictionary for Children.*

1. **fond**

_____

_____

2. **pride**

_____

_____

3. **reef**

_____

_____

4. **wit**

_____

_____

Name: _____

Review

Directions: Look at each question.
Follow the instructions.

1. Read the story. Underline the 2 sentences when you think Ann is happy. Box the one sentence when you think Ann is scared. Circle the one sentence when Ann is sad.

Ann is glad that she and Bill are in line to go on the roller coaster. Ann has never been on such a big ride before. She is biting her lip because she is nervous. Bill says he does not want to go with her. Ann does not want to go alone. She is not happy, but she gets out of the line with Bill. Bill changes his mind. "Yes, I do want to go," he says. Ann is glad her friend will go, too.

2. Circle the words that would be between **fly** and **game** in the dictionary.

   fog   forty   float   full   guess   gate   gave   gallon   forgot   fox

3. Read the dictionary entry for **gauze**. Then write a sentence using **gauze** in it.

gauze — a very thin, loosely woven cloth mostly used for bandages.

_____

_____

_____

_____

Name: _____

Finding Opposites

Directions: Read each sentence. Look at the word beside it. Complete the sentence with that word's antonym. Use words from the word box at the bottom of the page.

1. She got out of bed this morning very _____ . **early**

2. The Arctic Ocean is to the _____ . **south**

3. The elephant is _____ beside the mouse. **small**

4. When it rains it is _____ outside. **sunny**

5. The old dog was _____ because it had not eaten. **fat**

6. The clown looked sad. He wore a _____ on his face. **smile**

7. The _____ boy could easily reach the ball. **short**

8. The oven will _____ the bread if you do not turn it off. **freeze**

9. The two racers were close at the _____ of the race. **beginning**

10. Do not _____ the game without me. **finish**

11. The cotton made my pillow _____ . **hard**

12. I can jump the rope if it is _____ . **higher**

13. That clown looks _____ than the other one. **sadder**

14. I am sorry that I _____ the eggs. **carried**

15. My mother is a _____ . **child**

north	large	thin	late	grown-up	soft	lower	cloudy
frown	burn	tall	start	dropped	happier	end	

Finding Antonyms

Directions: Build the pyramids. Look at each sentence. Think of the antonym for the bold word. Now find the pyramid space where that word fits. Stack the antonyms on top of each other.

1. When I passed the test it was the **saddest** day of my life.
2. I **dropped** the dishes on the way to the kitchen.
3. You may play after you **start** the dishes.
4. My sister is **little** next to me.
5. He was **sad** because he won the prize.
6. How **short** was that snake that we saw?

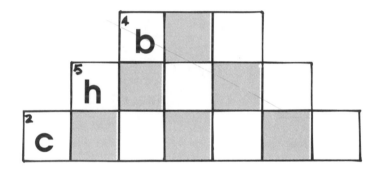

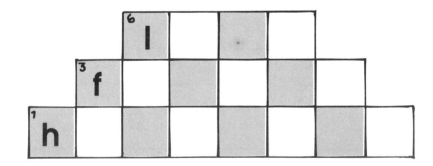

Name: _____

Finding Homonyms

Homonyms sound the same but have a different spelling and meaning.
Directions: Read each sentence. Finish each one with a word from the word box.

blew	night	blue	knight	hour	in	ant	inn
aunt	meet	too	two	to	beet		

1. A black _____ crawled up the wall.

2. It will be one _____ before we can go back home.

3. Will you _____ us then?

4. We plan to stay at an _____ during our trip.

5. The king had a _____ who rode the horses.

6. The wind _____ so hard that I almost lost my hat.

7. The color of his jacket was _____.

8. My _____ plans to visit us this week.

9. I will come _____ the house when it gets too cold outside.

10. It was late at _____ when we finally got there.

11. There will be _____ of us who will go.

12. I will mail a note _____ someone at the bank.

13. We grew a _____ in our garden.

14. We would like to join you _____.

Name: _____

Following Clues

Directions: Write the answer on the line beside each clue. Then circle the answer in the word puzzle.

```
k   n   i   g   h   t   i   n
p   h   o   u   r   i   f   f
a   n   t   w   a   i   t   d
u   p   d   e   e   r   q   e
n   i   n   i   n   n   n   a
t   o   o   g   o   a   r   r
m   e   e   h   i   g   h   i
n   e   w   t   n   i   s   t
```

CLUES

1. The name of a place where you stay on a trip. _____

2. The antonym of day. _____

3. 60 minutes is an _____.

4. The antonym of uncle. _____

5. You use scales to check this. _____

6. This bug is a pest. _____

7. What you do when you do not go ahead without someone.

   _____

8. An animal that runs swiftly. _____

9. Someone who can be found at a castle. _____

10. The antonym of out. _____

11. When something belongs to us. _____

12. A special name for someone. _____

Name: _____

Finding Synonyms

Directions: Look at the word on the left. Now draw a line to its synonym on the right. Synonyms are words with the same meanings.

infant	hello
forest	coat
bucket	grin
hi	baby
bunny	woods
cheerful	fall
jacket	repair
alike	small
smlle	same
autumn	hop
little	skinny
thin	top
jump	rabbit
shirt	pail
fix	happy

15

Name: _____

Finding Synonyms

Directions: Read each sentence. On the line beside it write a word from the word box that has the same meaning as the underlined word. The first one is done for you.

1. That animal is the **largest** one that I have ever seen. __**biggest**__

2. White mice are very **small** pets. _____

3. Gold fish move **fast** in the water. _____

4. The twins look exactly **the same**. _____

5. Leaves fall off of the trees in the **fall**. _____

6. Bambi was born in the **forest**. _____

7. We will go to the ocean on our next **vacation**. _____

8. The **bunny** hopped through the tall grass. _____

9. The **baby** was crying because he was hungry. _____

10. Put on your **coat** before you go outside. _____

11. Does that clown have a big **smile** on his face? _____

12. That was the **thinnest** man I have ever seen. _____

13. I will **repair** my bicycle as soon as I get home. _____

14. She was **bigger** than her sisters. _____

15. The children made **happy** sounds when they won. _____

```
    skinniest  biggest  jacket  little  quickly  woods
  grin  alike  trip  rabbit  fix  autumn  larger  infant  joyful
```

Kate Is Looking For Synonyms

Directions: Curious Kate is looking for synonyms. Look at the clues. Fill in the puzzle with a synonym for each clue.

Across
1. us
2. hop
3. skinny
4. jacket
5. top

Down
1. forest
2. coat
3. shirt
4. sleepy
5. kind

tired
jacket
top
woods
thin
we
shirt
coat
jump
nice

Name: _____

Review

Directions: Read each question. Follow the instructions.

1. These sentences do not make much sense. Fix each one by writing the antonym of the bold word in the space.

A. The old man fell **awake** while he ate his dinner. _____

B. She was the **saddest** one in the classroom. _____

C. The giraffe is the **shortest** animal at the zoo. _____

D. I did not mean to **fix** your new toy. _____

2. Circle the correct homonym for each sentence.

A. The child was **(pail or pale)** when she was sick.

B. It was a **(week or weak)** until our trip.

C. You can **(so or sew)** the apron onto the doll.

D. Our **(ant or aunt)** taught us this game.

3. Finish the sentence with a synonym of the bold word.

A. Please let me _____ the part that I broke. **repair**

B. I tried to carry the _____ of water. **bucket**

C. We will have pumpkins in our garden this _____. **fall**

D. The children at the birthday party were very _____. **cheerful**

4. Look at each set of words. Write A if they are antonyms, H if they are homonyms or S if they are synonyms.

_____ A. pail - pale   _____ E. wait - weight

_____ B. happy - cheerful   _____ F. too - two

_____ C. bucket - pail   _____ G. aunt - uncle

_____ D. coat - jacket   _____ H. knight - night

Follow Columbus' Trip To America!

Directions: Look at the map. Read the steps in his trip. Use a blue crayon to mark Christopher Columbus' path. Use a red crayon to show how he went back to Spain. Then answer the questions.

A long time ago many people thought the world was flat. Christopher Columbus believed it was round. In 1492 he set sail from Spain to prove it.

1. Christopher Columbus started in Spain.
2. He sailed across the Atlantic Ocean.
3. He landed in the West Indies.
4. Then he went back to Spain.

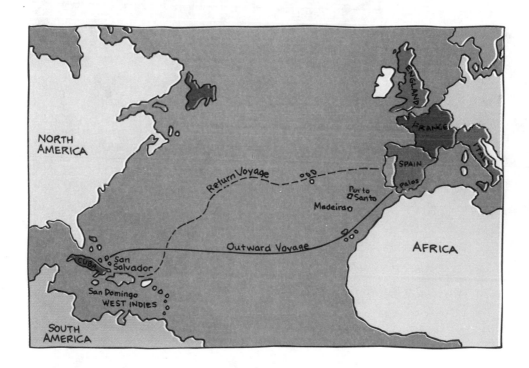

1. Where did Christopher Columbus start his trip? _____

2. Where did he land? _____

3. Did he go all around the world? _____

Name: _____

Follow Leif Eriksson

Directions: Many years before Christopher Columbus came to America there was another man who visited. Leif Eriksson was a Viking who also came to America by mistake.

Follow Leif Eriksson's trip with a red crayon. Read the steps that he took. Then answer the questions.

1. Leif Eriksson started in Norway.
2. He sailed across the Atlantic Ocean toward Greenland.
3. The wind blew him off his path. We think Leif Eriksson landed near where the United States and Canada touch.

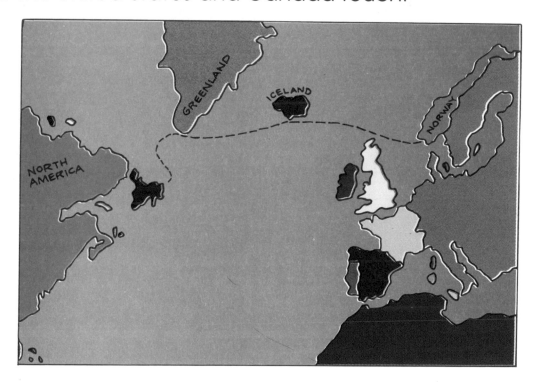

1. Where was Leif Eriksson trying to go? _____

2. What happened to his ship? _____

3. Where do we think he landed? _____

Let's Find America!

Directions: Pretend you are on your way to America. Use a red crayon to follow the path to find out how you get there.

1. Start in England and sail to France. **2.** From France sail to Spain.
3. From Spain go to the West Indies. **4.** From Spain sail to Iceland.
5. From Iceland go to the West Indies. **6.** From the West Indies sail to the United States. **7.** Use a purple crayon to make a better path from England to the United States.

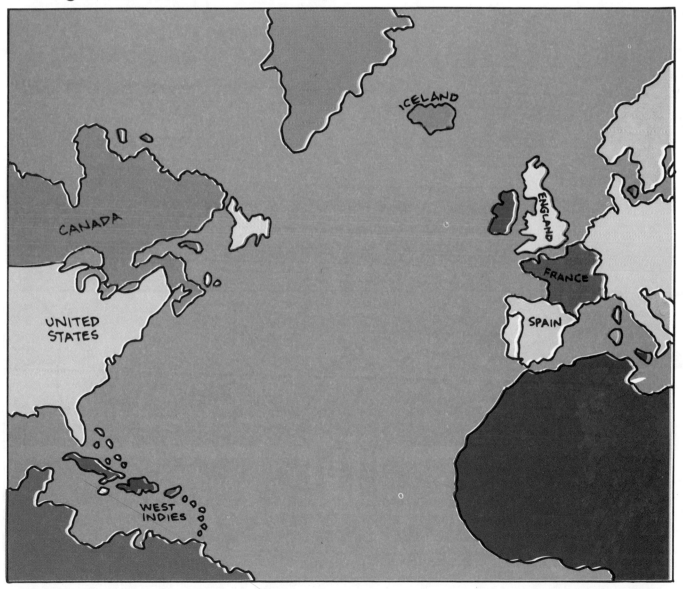

Name: _____

Going On A Trip

Directions: Ann's family is going on a trip. The map key will help you find where they are going.

Look at the map key. A map key helps you read a map. Find the things listed in the map key and color them on the map. Where is Ann's family going?

1. They went through a _____.

2. Over the _____.

3. Across the _____ tracks.

4. Over the _____.

5. To arrive at the _____.

MAP KEY
- ROAD
- RIVER
- TRAIN TRACKS
- MOUNTAINS
- WATER
- FOREST

Name: _____

Learning Map Skills

Directions: Look at the map key. Now draw a map of your neighborhood. Use the map key to help you find things to put on your map.

Name: _____

How Far Is It?

Directions: Miles show how far away one place is from another. Look at the map scale. It shows you that one inch equals one mile. Now use the map scale to find out how far Ann's home is from other places.

Map Scale

$\underline{\quad 1 \text{ inch} \quad}$ = 1 mile

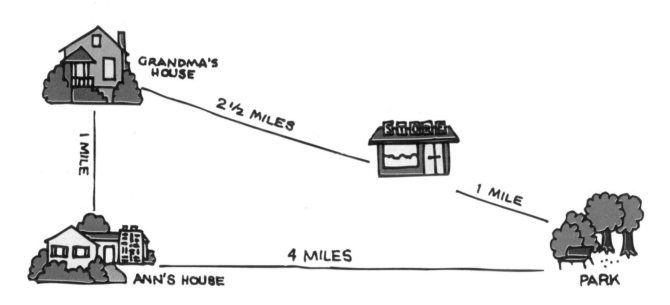

1. How far is it from Ann's house to the park? _____

2. How far is it from Ann's house to Grandma's house? _____

3. How far is it from Grandma's to the store? _____

4. How far did Ann go when she went from her house, to Grandma's, to the store? _____

Name: _____

Ann And Bill At The Playground

Directions: Ann and Bill are at the playground. Look at the map scale. Use a ruler to measure the map so you can answer the questions.

Map Scale

_____ = 1 foot

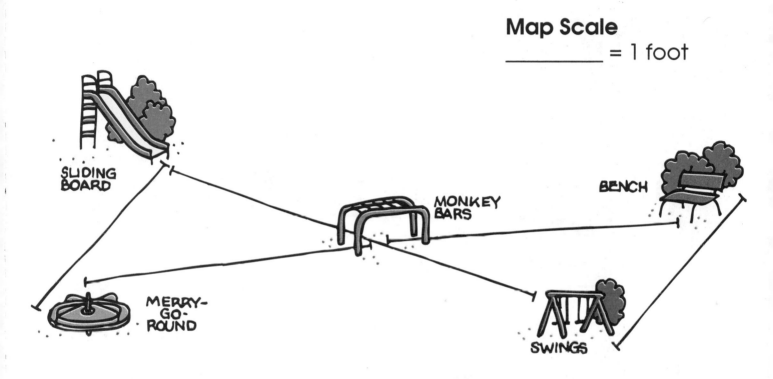

1. How far is it from the bench to the swings? _____

2. How far is it from the bench to the monkey bars? _____

3. How far is it from the monkey bars to the merry-go-round? _____

4. How far is it from the bench to the merry-go-round? _____

5. How far is it from the merry-go-round to the sliding board? _____

6. How far is it from the sliding board to the swings? _____

Review

Directions: Curious Kate knows that there is a treasure buried in the park. Use your new map skills to make her path. Answer the questions.

MAP KEY

SWINGS
WATER
BRIDGE
STOP SIGN
SAND PILE
BURIED TREASURE
HILL
BENCH

Clues

1. Curious Kate started at the swings.

2. She went over a bridge and to the stop sign.

3. She went up a hill and found a bench.

4. She went to the sand pile.

5. Where did she find the buried treasure? _____

Name: _____

Comparing Similarities

Directions: Analogies are made when things are compared to each other. Look at the example. Think about how each pair is related. Then finish the other analogies on this page.

EXAMPLE

1.

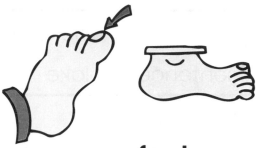

finger is to hand   as   toe is to ____**foot**____

2.

apple is to tree   as   flower is to _____

3.

tire is to car   as   wheel is to _____

4.

foot is to leg   as   hand is to _____

Name: _____

Making Analogies

Directions: Look at each analogy. Choose a word from the word box to finish it.

week	bottom	month	tiny
sentence	lake	out	eye

1. **up** is to **down**   as   **in** is to _____ **out** _____

2. **minute** is to **hour**   as   **day** is to _____

3. **month** is to **year**   as   **week** is to _____

4. **over** is to **under**   as   **top** is to _____

5. **big** is to **little**   as   **giant** is to _____

6. **sound** is to **ear**   as   **sight** is to _____

7. **page** is to **book**   as   **word** is to _____

8. **wood** is to **tree**   as   **water** is to _____

Name: _____

Finish Each Analogy

Directions: Finish each analogy with a word from the word box.

dog	fish	cup	left	south	cat
light	bear	small	arm	zoo	evening

1. **hive** is to **bee**   as   **dog house** is to **dog** _____

2. **up** is to **down**   as   **right** is to _____

3. **lamb** is to **sheep**   as   **kitten** is to _____

4. **big** is to **little**   as   **large** is to _____

5. **black** is to **white**   as   **dark** is to _____

6. **day** is to **night**   as   **morning** is to _____

7. **knee** is to **leg**   as   **elbow** is to _____

8. **chicken** is to **farm**   as   **monkey** is to _____

9. **fork** is to **spoon**   as   **glass** is to _____

10. **wing** is to **bird**   as   **fin** is to_____

11. **feather** is to **duck**   as   **fur** is to _____

12. **east** is to **west**   as   **north** is to _____

Name: _____

Finish Each Analogy

Directions: Finish the analogy with a word from the word box.

finish	less	pony	oven	finger	big
week	hour	cat	weak	under	little

1. **second** is to **minute** as   **minute** is to _____hour_____

2. **fast** is to **slow**   as   **big** is to _____

3. **child** is to **mother**   as   **kitten** is to _____

4. **puppy** is to **kitten**   as   **calf** is to _____

5. **less** is to **more**   as   **little** is to _____

6. **freeze** is to **freezer**   as   **bake** is to _____

7. **late** is to **early**   as   **more** is to _____

8. **first** is to **last**   as   **start** is to _____

9. **in** is to **out**   as   **over** is to _____

10. **hard** is to **soft**   as   **strong** is to _____

11. **earring** is to **ear**   as   **ring** is to _____

12. **hour** is to **day**   as   **day** is to _____

Name: _____

Putting Things In Order

Directions: Look at each question. The two words there suggest an order called a sequence. Choose a word from the word box to finish the sequence. Be careful. There are more words in the word box than you need. The first one is done for you.

| below | three | fifteen | December | twenty | under |
| after | go | third | hour | March | yard |

1. January, February,   **March**_____

2. before, during,   _____

3. over, on,   _____

4. come, stay,   _____

5. second, minute,   _____

6. first, second,   _____

7. five, ten,   _____

8. inch, foot,   _____

Sequencing

Directions: Look at each group of words. The sequence is mixed up. Unscramble the sequence so that it is from least to most.

EXAMPLE:

minute, second, hour   **second, minute, hour**

1. least, most, more   _____

2. full, empty, half-full   _____

3. month, day, year   _____

4. baseball, golf ball, soccer ball   _____

5. penny, dollar, quarter   _____

6. $4.12, $3.18, $3.22   _____

7. boy, man, infant   _____

8. mother, daughter, grandmother   _____

Name: _____

Sequencing

Directions: Look at each group of words. The sequence is mixed. Unscramble the sequence so that it is from largest to smallest.

1. small, medium, large   _____

2. toddler, baby, child   _____

3. year, minute, day   _____

4. $5.50, $6.25, $5.75   _____

5. thirty, ten, twenty   _____

6. gallon, quart, pint   _____

7. half, quarter, whole   _____

8. most, least, same   _____

Review

Directions: Read each question. Follow the instructions.

1. Match the analogy on the left with the similar one on the right.

finger is to **hand**	**east** is to **west**
hard is to **soft**	**toe** is to **foot**
left is to **right**	**over** is to **under**
top is to **bottom**	**strong** is to **weak**

2. Finish each analogy.

minute is to **hour**	as	**day** is to _____
up is to **down**	as	**high** is to _____
black is to **white**	as	**night** is to _____
good is to **bad**	as	**right** is to _____

3. Complete each sequence.

April, May, _____

first, second, _____

boy, father, _____

yesterday, today, _____

4. Unscramble the sequences. The order should be smallest to largest.

large, small, medium _____

middle, last, first _____

empty, full, half-full _____

hour, second, minute _____

34

Name: _____

Classifying

Directions: Look at the words in the word box. Each word can be grouped with a season. Fill in the pyramids for each season with a word from the word box.

July 4	hot	football	bike rides	windy	leaves
kite	froze	sled ride	swimming	Thanksgiving	
snowman	bunnies	ice	jack-o-lantern	baseball	

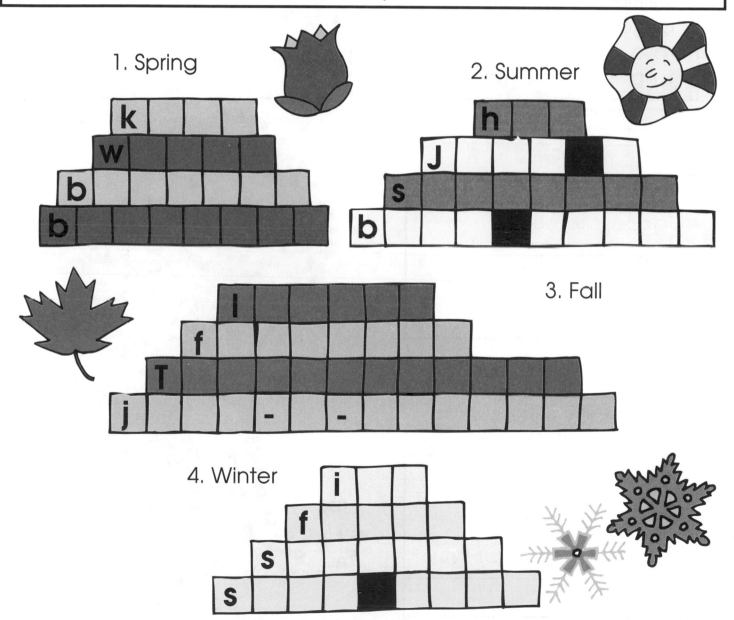

1. Spring

k
w
b
b

2. Summer

h
J
s
b

3. Fall

l
f
T
j - -

4. Winter

i
f
s
s

Name: _____

Help Mrs. Posey

Directions: Mrs. Posey is sorting out the names of birds from the names of the trees and the flowers. Move each word from the word box to its right place. Put 4 words in each box.

Birds

robin	elm
buckeye	willow
sunflower	bluejay
canary	oak
rose	wren
tulip	morning glory

Trees

Flowers

36

Name: _____

Animal Stories

Directions: Read each animal story. Then look at the fun facts. Beside each fact put an H for horse, P for panda or D for Dog.

Horses

Horses are fun to ride. You can ride them in the woods or in fields. Horses usually have pretty names. Sometimes, if they are golden, they are called Amber. When it is hot they swish their tails. That keeps the flies away from them.

Pandas

Pandas are from China. They like to climb trees. They scratch bark to write messages to their friends in the trees. When Pandas get hungry, they gnaw on bamboo shoots!

Dogs

Dogs are good pets. A lot of times people call them names like Spot or Fido. Sometimes they are named after their looks. For example, a brown dog is sometimes named Brownie. Some people have special, small doors for their dogs to use.

Fun Facts

_____ 1. My name is often Spot or Fido.

_____ 2. I am from China.

_____ 3. Snoopy is my friend.

_____ 4. I like to carry people into the fields.

_____ 5. My favorite food is bamboo.

_____ 6. Flies bother me when I am hot.

_____ 7. Amber is often my name when I am golden.

_____ 8. I leave messages for my friends by scratching bark.

_____ 9. Sometimes I have my own special door on a house.

Name: _____

People Of Wackyville

Directions: Compare the people of Wackyville to each other. Read the first sentence. Think about it. Then read the second sentence. Answer the question. The first one is done for you.

1. Wanda cooks fast. Joe cooks faster than Wanda.
   Who cooks the fastest? _____**Joe**_____

2. Mr. Green plants many flowers. Mrs. Posey plants more.
   Who plants the most? _____

3. Joe weighs a lot. Edward weighs more.
   Who weighs the most? _____

4. Sheila is young. Billy is younger.
   Who is the youngest? _____

5. Ms. Brown has many trees. Mr. Smith has more.
   Who has the most? _____

6. Leo says his pie is good. Mindy says hers is better.
   Whose pie is the best? _____

7. Save Right has many toys. Play Time has more.
   Which store has the most toys? _____

8. An elephant moves slow. A turtle moves slower.
   Which one is the slowest? _____

Making Deductions

Directions: Carefully read each sentence. Answer the question.

1. Bob is tall. Jim is taller than Bob. Lee is taller than Jim. Who is the tallest?

_____

2. Brett was happy. Jenny was happier than Brett. Roger was happier than Jenny. Who was the happiest?

_____

3. An orange weighs a lot. A grapefruit weighs more than an orange. A watermelon weighs more than grapefruit. What weighs the most?

_____

4. Mark shot many baskets. Ted shot more baskets than Mark. Ed shot more than Ted. Who shot the most baskets?

_____

5. Mandy liked the movie. Teresa liked the movie more than Mandy. Liz liked the movie more than Teresa. Who liked the movie most?

_____

6. Jane danced fast. Duane danced faster than Jane. Luann danced faster than Duane. Who danced the fastest?

_____

7. The balloon floated high. The bubble went higher than the balloon. The airplane was higher than the bubble. What was the highest?

_____

8. The kitten was small. The mouse was smaller than the kitten. The bird was smaller than the mouse. What was the smallest?

_____

Name: _____

Hunting For Holly

Directions: Ann's pet dog, Holly, has disappeared. Help Ann and her friends find Holly.

Look at the picture of Ann's house. Then read the clues. Write the person's name on the line in the room where they were.

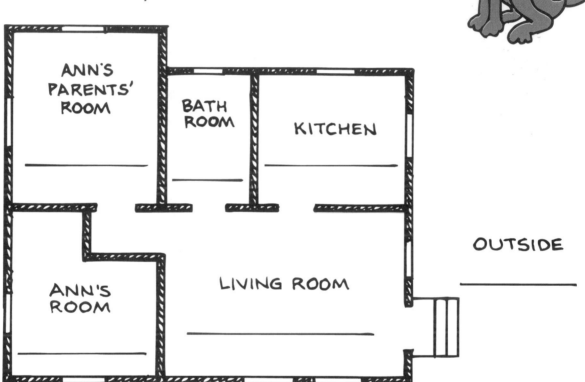

1. Holly is not under Ann's bed. Ann was in her room and she did not see Holly go there.
2. Holly is not outside because Paul was in the yard.
3. Ann's mother was in the kitchen. Holly is not there.
4. Ann's father was in the room next to the kitchen. He was not in the bathroom. He did not see Holly either.
5. Holly never goes in the bathroom. She is afraid of the water.
6. Holly cannot leave the yard. There is a fence around it.
7. Where is Holly? _____

40

Name: _____

The Winning Hit

Directions: Read the story. Use the softball diamond to find out who made the winning hit. Write the players' names on the line where they were.

Ann and her friends are playing a game of softball. The score is tied. The luck of the next batter will decide who wins the game. Ann's team includes Bill, John, Jane, Mary and Martha.

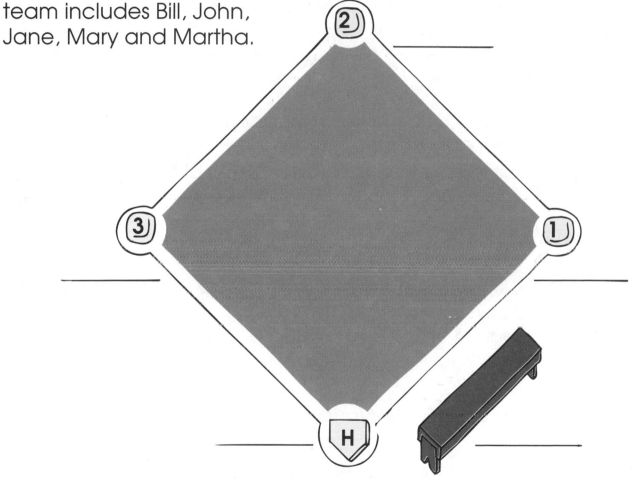

1. Martha just made a run. She sits down on the bench to rest.
2. John is on third base waiting to run.
3. Jane and Mary are on the other two bases.
4. Bill hurt his arm. He can not hit this time.
5. The last batter hits the ball hard. John runs to home plate. Ann's team has won. Who was the last batter?

Review

Directions: Look at each question. Follow the instructions.

1. Read each paragraph. Then look at the Fun Facts. Decide if each fact describes potato chips, a hot dog or a popsicle. Put C for potato chips, H for hot dog or P for popsicle.

Potato Chips

Once upon a time a man was eating french fries. He thought they were too soggy. When he sent them back to the chef, the chef cut some potatos very thin and fried them. These were the first potato chips!

Hot Dogs

Hot dogs have not always been called hot dogs. A long time ago people only called them frankfurters. But an artist who was at a baseball game drew a picture of frankfurter and put it on a bun. He made the frankfurter look like a dog! Then he wrote "hot dog" under his picture!

Popsicles

One cold night in 1905 a man named Frank Epperson left a glass of lemonade on a windowsill. It had a stirring stick in it. The lemonade froze and the first popsicle was born. But the popsicle was called an Epsicle at first.

_____ They used to be called frankfurters.

_____ A chef sliced them thin and fried them.

_____ The first one was made of frozen lemonade.

_____ The first picture of one of these was drawn at a baseball game.

_____ It was first called the Epsicle after Frank Epperson who invented it.

_____ A customer thought his french fries were too soggy.

_____ The person who named them thought they looked like dogs.

_____ It was invented in 1905 with a glass and a stick.

Name: _____

The Jitterbug

Directions: Read about the jitterbug. Then answer the questions.

The music is playing loudly. Paul and Mary are facing each other. They hold hands. They are going to do something called the jitterbug. Paul starts bouncing back and forth, first on one foot, then on the other. Mary starts doing the same thing. They are "keeping time" to the music's beat. Then they start moving around a lot. Mary ducks under Paul's arm. They are laughing because they are having fun.

1. What are Paul and Mary doing? _____
_____
_____

2. Why are they bouncing back and forth, first on one foot then on the other?
_____
_____
_____

3. Why are Paul and Mary laughing?
_____
_____
_____

Name: _____

Mrs. Posey's Colorful Yard!

Directions: Read the story. Answer the questions.

Mrs. Posey plants roses everywhere. She plants yellow roses near her front porch. She plants red roses near the back door. There are also pink roses and white roses in her yard. Every time the mailman comes to her house he sneezes. "You should not plant so many flowers," he tells Mrs. Posey. Mrs. Posey just smiles.

1. What are Mrs. Posey's favorite flowers? _____

_____

_____

2. Why do you think the mailman tells Mrs. Posey, "You should not plant so many flowers."

_____

_____

_____

3. Why does Mrs. Posey smile?

_____

_____

_____

Mrs. Posey Gets Hurt

Directions: Read about Mrs. Posey again. Then answer the questions.

Mrs. Posey is working in her rose garden. She is trimming the branches so that the plants will grow better. Mrs. Posey is careful because rose bushes have thorns on them. "Hello, Mrs. Posey," calls Ann as she rides her bicycle down the street. "Hi, Ann," she calls back. Then she yells, "Ouch." She runs inside the house and stays there for a few minutes. When Mrs. Posey comes outside she has a bandage on one finger.

1. Why is Mrs. Posey careful when she works with rose bushes?

_____

_____

_____

2. Why does Mrs. Posey look up from her work?

_____

_____

_____

3. Why did Mrs. Posey say, "Ouch?"

_____

_____

_____

4. Why did Mrs. Posey run into the house?

_____

_____

_____

Name: _____

Something Is Hiding!

Directions: Read about cocoons. Then answer the questions.

Some people do not like caterpillars. They look like fuzzy worms. They have many legs and they creep and crawl on trees and leaves. But a caterpillar is really the beginning of something else. It eats leaves for many days. After it is very big it spins a cocoon. It stays inside for a few months. When the cocoon opens something else is inside. It is very beautiful. It flies away.

1. Why does the caterpillar eat leaves for many days?

_____

_____

2. What happens while the caterpillar is in the cocoon?

_____

_____

3. When does the cocoon open?

_____

_____

4. What comes out of the cocoon?

_____

_____

_____

Name: _____

Butterflies Protect Themselves!

Directions: Read about butterflies. Then answer the questions.

Butterflies are many different colors. They have different designs on them, too. These colors and designs help them. When some butterflies are resting they look like leaves. Animals cannot see them. Other butterflies smell funny. Animals do not like the smell.

1. How do the different colors and designs help protect butterflies?

_____

_____

_____

2. What do they need protection from?

_____

_____

_____

3. Why do some butterflies look like leaves?

_____

_____

_____

4. Why do some butterflies smell funny?

_____

_____

_____

Name: _____

Eskimos Of Long Ago

Directions: Read about Eskimos. Then answer the questions.

Eskimos live in Alaska. A long time ago Eskimos lived in houses made of snow, dirt or animal skins. They moved around from place to place a lot. The Eskimos hunted and fished. Often they ate raw meat because they had no way to cook it. When they ate it raw, they liked it dried or frozen. Eskimos used animal skin for their clothes. They used fat from whales, seals and other animals to heat their houses.

1. Why did the Eskimos make houses out of snow?

_____

_____

2. How did they use animal fat to heat their houses?

_____

_____

3. Why did they eat their meat raw?

_____

_____

Name: _____

Eskimos Have Changed!

Directions: Read about today's Eskimos. Then answer the questions.

Today, many Eskimos stay in villages instead of always moving around. They work in jobs, instead of hunting and fishing. Eskimo children go to school, too. Their houses are heated from oil out of the ground, instead of animal oil. Many Eskimos use snowmobiles instead of dogs and sleds. In the winter they wear coats that are very warm.

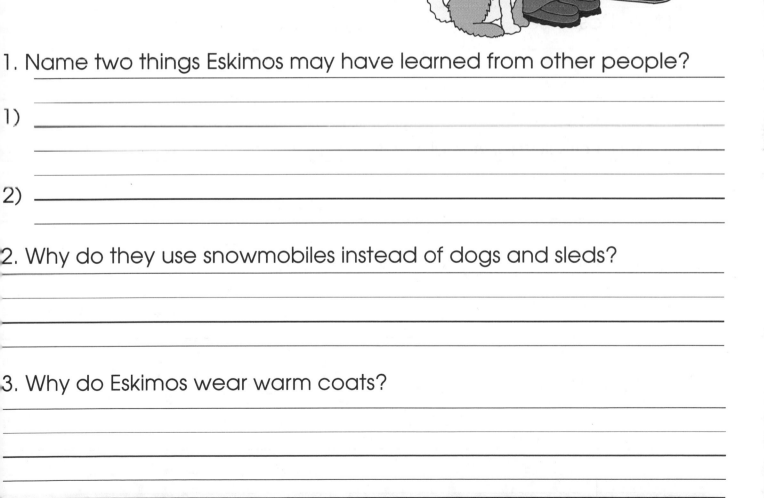

1. Name two things Eskimos may have learned from other people?

1) _____

   _____

2) _____

   _____

2. Why do they use snowmobiles instead of dogs and sleds?

_____

_____

3. Why do Eskimos wear warm coats?

_____

_____

_____

Review

Directions: Read about Mrs. Posey's adventure. Answer the questions.

It is wintertime. Mrs. Posey is going to Alaska. She has decided to fly there in an airplane. Mrs. Posey wonders what kind of clothes she should pack for her trip. She sees Alaska on the map and it is very close to the north pole. Mrs. Posey is not sure if she will like this vacation.

1. What will the weather be like in Alaska? _____

2. Will Mrs. Posey see any flowers in Alaska?

_____

_____

_____

3. What kind of clothes should Mrs. Posey take?

_____

_____

4. Do you think Mrs. Posey will ride a snowmobile in Alaska?

_____

_____

5. Would you like to go to Alaska in the wintertime?

_____

_____

Name: _____

Learning How To Use The Library

Directions: A library is a place that has many books. People can borrow the books and read them. Then they take them back to the library.

Most libraries have two sections. One is for adults' books and one is for children's books. A librarian is there to help people find books.

Read the title of each library book. On the line under each title write A if you think it is an adult's book or C if you think it is a children's book.

1. *Sam Squirrel Goes to the City*

    _____

2. *Barney Beagle Plays Baseball*

    _____

3. *Charlotte's Web*

    _____

4. *Understanding Your Child*

    _____

5. *Curious George*

    _____

6. *The Tale of Peter Rabbit*

7. *The Selling of the President*

    _____

8. *Jenny's First Party*

    _____

Introducing Library Skills

Directions: Sometimes you can tell if a book is fiction or nonfiction just by its name.

Fiction books are storybooks. They include stories that a writer has made up. An example of a fiction book is *Baseball Mouse*. Nonfiction books are books that have information or facts in them. An example of a nonfiction book is *Animals of Long Ago*. Both adults and children read fiction and nonfiction books.

Look at each book title below. Underline the titles that could be fiction books. Circle the titles that could be nonfiction.

1. *Libraries and How to Use Them*

2. *Animals of Long Ago*

3. *Sylvester and the Magic Pebble*

4. *Sam Squirrel Goes to the City*

5. *Easy Microwave Cooking for Kids*

6. *Talking Animal Tales!*

7. *Treasure Island*

8. *Maps and Globes*

Name: _____

Finding Books In A Library

Directions: Fiction books in a library are filed in ABC order using the author's last name.

Example: Jack Ezra Keats would be Keats, Jack Ezra.

Nonfiction books are grouped by subjects. For example, all books about snakes are grouped together and all books about outer space are grouped together.

Practice filing books in ABC order. Here is a list of author's names. On the line beside the name put the number of where that book would come in ABC order.

_____ Rand, Ann and Paul

_____ Burton, Virginia Lee

_____ Keats, Ezra Jack

_____ Rey, H. A.

_____ Irving, Washington

_____ Lionni, Leo

_____ Potter, Beatrix

_____ Blume, Judy

Name: _____

Encyclopedias And Dictionaries

Directions: Reference books are books that tell you basic facts. Dictionaries and encyclopedias are reference books. You usually are not allowed to take reference books out of the library.

Dictionaries tell you about words. Encyclopedias give you other information, such as when the president was born, what the Civil War was, and where Eskimos live. Encyclopedias usually come in sets of more than 20 books. Information is listed in ABC order, just like words are listed in the dictionary.

There are other kinds of reference books, too. Those can include books of maps, called atlases. Reference books are hardly ever read cover to cover.

Read each fact. Draw a line from the fact to the book that you would use to find it. Is it about a dictionary or is it about an encyclopedia? The first one is done for you.

1. I would have the definition of **divide** in me.
2. I would tell you when George Washington was born.
3. I would give you the correct spelling for many words.
4. I would tell you where Indians live.
5. I would tell you the names of many butterflies.
6. I would tell you what **modern** means.
7. I would give you the history of dinosaurs.
8. If you have to write a paper about Eskimos, I could help you.

Name: _____

Periodicals

Directions: Learn about magazines and newspapers.

Magazines and newspapers are called periodicals. Libraries usually have some of them, too.

There are many kinds of magazines. Some tell you about children. Others have recipes in them. Some magazines have information about the world in them. There is even a magazine about Nintendo!

Almost every city and town has a newspaper. Newspapers can come out every day or every week or every month. Newspapers tell you what is happening in your town and in the world. They have sections about sports and about clothes. They give you a lot of information.

Look at each question. Follow the instructions.

1. Find a magazine that you would like to look through. What is its name?

_____

List the names of three stories in the magazine.

1. _____

2. _____

3. _____

2. Now look at a newspaper. What is its name?

_____

The titles of newspaper stories are called headlines. What are some of the headlines in your newspaper.

1. _____

2. _____

Paul And Mary Go To The Library

Directions: Paul and Mary are going to the library to get some facts about the moon. Where should they look while they are there?

Answer the questions to help Paul and Mary find out where they can get information about the moon at the library.

1. Should they look in the children's section or in the adults' section? _____

2. Should they look for a fiction book or a nonfiction book? _____

3. Who at the library can help them? _____

4. What reference book should they look in? _____

5. Where else can they look for information that may have been in the news? _____

6. What word would they look up in the encyclopedia to get the information that they need? _____

Name: _____

Puzzling Out Library Terms

Directions: Read each clue. Use some of the words from the word box to finish the crossword puzzle.

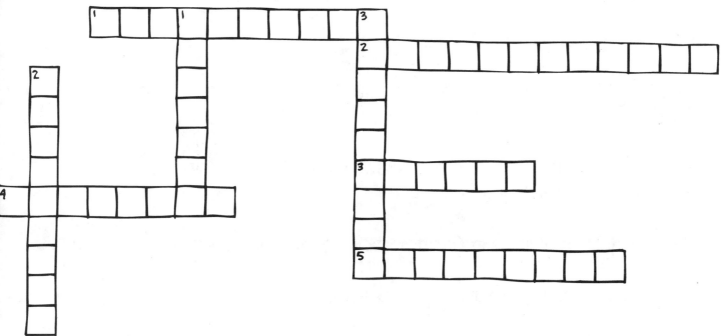

reference   nonfiction   adults'   fiction   children   newspaper   library   magazine   librarian   encyclopedia   dictionary   periodicals

Across

1. A story based on facts is_____.
2. You could find out when Abraham Lincoln died in this book.
3. If you are not in the children's section, then you may be in the ___ section.
4. This is called a periodical.
5. Dictionaries and encyclopedias are included in these.

Down

1. A story that someone has made up is ____.
2. If you cannot find what you are looking for you should ask this person.
3. This can be delivered to your house everyday.

Review

Directions: Circle each answer.

1. A book containing only facts about outer space is a (fiction or nonfiction) book.

2. Books are sometimes listed in (ABC or 123) order according to their authors' names.

3. A book with the title, *The Ghost of Windy Hill,* is probably (fiction or nonfiction).

4. An encyclopedia is a (periodical or reference) book.

5. Newspapers and magazines are called (references or periodicals).

6. (True or False) I can keep books that I get from the library forever.

7. List three things that you can find in an encyclopedia.

1) _____

2) _____

3) _____

8. List these authors in ABC order the way they would appear in the library: H.A. Rey, Lucy Ozone and Margaret Ott.
   (Hint: Last names come first.)

1) _____

2) _____

3) _____

Name: _____

Our President, The Inventor!

Directions: Read the story about Thomas Jefferson.
Answer the questions.

Thomas Jefferson was the third president of the United States. He was also an inventor. That means he had new ideas for things that he made that had never been made before.

Thomas Jefferson made many inventions. He built a chair that rotated in circles. He also built a rotating music stand. One interesting invention was a walking stick that unfolded into a chair. Thomas Jefferson invented a new kind of plow for farming, too.

1. The main idea is: (circle one)

   Thomas Jefferson was very busy when he was president.
   Thomas Jefferson was a president and an inventor.

2. Who is a person who has new ideas for things that they make that no one else has made before?

   _____

3. List 3 inventions of Thomas Jefferson.

   _____
1) _____
   _____
2) _____
   _____
3) _____
   _____

Name: _____

Inventing The Bicycle!

Directions: Read the story about the bicycle. Then answer the questions.

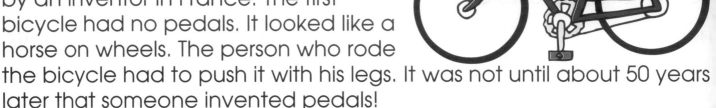

In 1790 one of the first bicycles was made. It was made all of wood by an inventor in France. The first bicycle had no pedals. It looked like a horse on wheels. The person who rode the bicycle had to push it with his legs. It was not until about 50 years later that someone invented pedals!

Bikes became much more popular in the United States during the 1890s. Streets and parks were full of people riding them. Still, though, they were not like the bicycles we ride today. They had heavier tires and the brakes and lights weren't very good. Bicycling is still very popular in the United States. Biking is good exercise for you and it is still a good way of transportation!

1. Who invented the bicycle? _____

2. What did it look like? _____

3. When did bikes become popular in the United States? _____

4. Where did people ride them? _____

5. Why is biking good for you? _____

6. How long have bikes been popular in the United States? _____

Name: _____

Discovering Chewing Gum!

Directions: Read about chewing gum. Then answer the questions.

Thomas Adams was an inventor in the United States. In 1870 he was looking for something that could replace rubber. He was working with chicle ("chick-ul") that comes from a certain kind of tree in Mexico. Years ago Mexicans chewed chicle.

Thomas Adams decided to try it! He liked it so much he started selling it. About 20 years later he owned a big factory that made chewing gum.

1. Who was the United States inventor who started selling chewing gum? _____

2. What was he hoping to invent? _____

3. When did he invent chewing gum? _____

4. Where does the chicle come from? _____

5. Why did Thomas Adams start selling chewing gum? _____

6. How long was it until he owned a big factory selling chewing gum? _____

Name: _____

The Peaceful Pueblos

Directions: Read about the Pueblo Native Americans. Answer the questions.

The Pueblos ("Pooh-eb-low") live in the southwest United States in New Mexico and Arizona. They have lived there for hundreds of years. The Pueblos have always been peaceful Native Americans. They never started wars. They only fought if they were attacked first.

The Pueblos loved to dance. Even their dances were peaceful. They danced when they asked the gods for rain or sunshine. They danced for other reasons, too. Sometimes the Pueblos wore masks when they danced.

1. The main idea is: (circle one)

   Pueblos are peaceful Native Americans who still live in part of the United States.

   Pueblo Native Americans never started wars.

2. Do Pueblos like to fight?

3. What do the Pueblos like to do? _____

Name: _____

Homes Made Of Clay!

Directions: Read about adobe houses. Then answer the questions.

Pueblo Native Americans live in houses made of clay. They are called adobe ("ah-doe-bee") houses. Adobe is a yellow-colored clay that comes from the ground. The hot sun in New Mexico and Arizona helps dry the clay to make strong bricks. The Pueblos have used adobe to build their homes for many years.

Pueblos use adobe for other reasons, too. The women in the tribes make beautiful pottery out of adobe. While the clay is damp they make it into shapes. After they have made their bowls and other containers, they paint them with lively designs.

1. Who is this story about? _____

2. What are their houses made out of? _____

3. When did they start building adobe houses? _____

4. Where do they get the adobe? _____

5. Why do adobe bricks need to be dried? _____

6. How do they make pottery from adobe? _____

Name: _____

Review

Directions: Read the story about George Washington. Then answer the questions.

George Washington was the first president. An old story said that he was very honest. It said that when he was six years old he cut down a cherry tree on the farm where he lived. The story said Washington could not lie about it. He told his dad he cut down the tree. But George Washington did not chop down a cherry tree. People have found out that this story was made up by someone else. They say a man named Parson Weems wrote one of the first books about George Washington. He liked Washington so much he made up that story.

1. The main idea of this story is:

    George Washington cut down a cherry tree.

    George Washington did not cut down a cherry tree.

2. Is the story of George Washington chopping down a cherry tree (true or false)? (circle one)

3. Who made up the story about George Washington? _____

4. When did the story say George Washington cut down the tree? _____

5. Where was the tree that the story said he cut down? _____

6. How did Parson Weems tell people the story? _____

The Wrong Words

Read this story about a lion and a mouse.
As you read, you will find nine words that do not belong.
Write the words in order at the bottom of the page.

One day in the jungle, a big lion grabbed a little mouse. The lion held the mouse in his paws.

The mouse looked up at the lion and your said, "Please let me go. I am too little to be a good meal. And if you heart let me go, someday I will help you."

The lion laughed, "You help beats me! What a silly idea." The lion one laughed so hard, that it let the mouse slip away. The mouse ran home.

Several weeks hundred passed by. The mouse was at home fixing thousand dinner for his wife. Suddenly, he heard the lion roaring in pain. The mouse ran from his house. He ran through the times woods. He found the lion stuck in a rope trap. The lion every pulled at the ropes, but couldn't get free.

The mouse said, "I'll save you, friend lion."

The little mouse started chewing on the ropes. Soon one rope had a big hole in it. Then another rope had a hole. Then another and another. In a few minutes, the lion was day free. The lion smiled at the mouse and said, "You are little, but you saved the king of the beasts. Thank you, my special friend."

This is a fact. _____ _____ _____

_____ _____ _____ _____

_____ _____!

Who Can It Be?

Think of all the people you know.
Think of friends and relatives.
Think of characters from books, movies, and TV.
Try to think of just the right person
for each sentence below.
When you have the right person in mind,
write the person's name on the blank line.

1. _____ runs as fast as a cheetah.

2. _____ has a voice like a police siren.

3. _____ plays like a silly kitten.

4. _____ can be as quiet as a pillow.

5. _____ is as strong as a polar bear.

6. _____ is as smart as an encyclopedia.

7. _____ is as friendly as a puppy greeting its master.

8. _____ can get as nervous as a rabbit.

9. _____ dresses in colors like a rainbow.

10. _____ can be as sneaky as a fox.

Understanding similes

This Leads to That

Think of three words that have to do with the word <u>circus</u>.
Write them on these lines.

_____   _____

_____

Choose one of your three words. | A |
Write it in box **A** at the right.
Write three other words that go with the word in box **A**.

_____   _____

_____

Choose a word from your second list. | B |
Write it in box **B** at the right.
Write three other words that go with the word in box **B**.
Do not use any words you used before.

_____   _____

_____

Choose a word from your third list. | C |
Write it in box **C** at the right.
Write three other words that go with the word in box **C**.
Do not use any words you used before.

_____   _____

_____

Look at all the words you wrote.
Try to make a sentence using at least one word
from each of your lists.

_____

_____

Using related words

Shared Thinking

Have a friend do this activity with you.
For **Round 1**, you and your friend think of the word <u>baseball</u>.
Do not talk to each other.
On this page, write six baseball words that come into your mind.
Your friend writes six words on another sheet of paper.
Do not show each other your papers until you are finished.
When you both are finished, compare your lists.
Score 1 point for every word that is on both lists.
Each of you write your score at the bottom of your own list.
Play **Round 2** for <u>school</u> and **Round 3** for <u>Halloween</u> in the same way.

Round 1 Baseball	Round 2 School	Round 3 Halloween
_____	_____	_____
_____	_____	_____
_____	_____	_____
_____	_____	_____
_____	_____	_____
_____	_____	_____
Score _____	Score _____	Score _____

How many points did you score in all? _____
Eleven to 18 points means you and your friend have
thoughts that agree nearly perfectly.
Five to 10 points means you and your friend almost
always think alike.
One to 4 points means you and your friend have ideas
that are sometimes alike.
Zero means you and your friend are on different wavelengths.
You can do this activity again with three new words
or with another partner.

Using related words

68

What Will Happen?

Here is part of a story about Julian who has a loose tooth.

"Well," my father said, "if you wait long enough, it will fall out." He was talking about my tooth, my right bottom front tooth.

"How long do I have to wait?" I asked. Because I had *two* right bottom front teeth—one firm little new one pushing in, and one wiggly old one.

"I can't say," my father said. "Maybe a month, maybe two months. Maybe less."

"I don't want to wait," I said. "I want *one* tooth there, and I don't want to wait two months!"

"All right!" said my father. "I'll take care of it!" He jumped out of his chair and ran out the door to the garage. He was back in a minute, carrying something—a pair of pliers!

"Your tooth is a little loose already," my father said. "So I'll just put the pliers in your mouth for a second, twist, and the tooth will come out. You won't feel a thing!"

"I won't feel a thing?" I looked at the pliers—huge, black-handled pliers with a long pointed tip. I thought I *would* feel a thing. I thought it would hurt.

"Shall I?" said my dad. He raised the pliers toward my mouth.

What do you think will happen next?
Write your ideas here or on another sheet of paper.

_____

_____

Do you want to know what really happens?
You can find out in the book *The Stories Julian Tells* by Ann Cameron.

Predicting outcomes

Crime Buster

Mrs. Glow's biggest diamond is missing.
Here are four police reports.
Read each one.
Then fill in the Crime Buster Sheet.

Police Log   Captain Smith

8:15 PM - Mrs. Glow called to report a stolen diamond. Three diamond thieves are in town - Diamond Bugs, Diamond Stan, and Unlucky Lou. I sent Detectives Shin, Gomez, and Foster to investigate.

Police Log   Detective Shin

7:30 PM - Last time Mrs. Glow saw the diamond.
7:50 PM - Butler heard noises in Mrs. Glow's room.
8:00 PM - Cook saw a red car speeding away from house.

Police Log   Detective Foster

Bugs and Stan drive red cars. Lou has a blue car.
7:00 - 8:30 PM - Bugs had dinner at the Drippy Diner and then left.
8:30 PM - Lou walked in and took a seat.

Police Log   Detective Gomez

4:00 PM - Stan went to store to buy a present for his wife's birthday.
4:30 - 9:30 PM - Stan was at wife's party.
5:00 PM - Lou borrowed Stan's car.
10:00 PM - Lou returned Stan's car and gave flowers to Stan's wife.

Crime Buster Sheet

1. What time was the robbery? _____

2. What color car was the robber driving? _____

3. Who has that color car? _____

4. What was Bugs doing at the time of the robbery? _____

5. What was Stan doing at the time of the robbery? _____

6. Who was driving Stan's car? _____

7. What was Lou doing? _____

8. Whom should Police Captain Smith arrest? _____

Organizing information

Three Poems

Read each poem. Then answer the question below it.

Way Down South

Way down South where bananas grow,
A grasshopper stepped on an elephant's toe.
The elephant said with tears in his eyes,
"Pick on somebody your own size!"

What nonsense is in this poem? _____

_____

As I Was Going Out

As I was going out one day
My head fell off and rolled away.
But when I saw that it was gone,
I picked it up and put it on.

And when I got into the street
A fellow cried: "Look at your feet!"
I looked at them and sadly said:
"I've left them both asleep in bed!"

HEY!
I

What is silly in this poem? _____

_____

Hullabaloo

I raised a great hullabaloo
When I found a large mouse in my stew,
    Said the waiter, "Don't shout
    And wave it about,
Or the rest will be wanting one, too!"

Why is this poem funny? _____

_____

Identifying inconsistencies

How I Felt

Remember a time you felt excited.
What happened to make you feel excited?

_____

_____

_____

Remember a time you laughed.
What happened to make you laugh?

_____

_____

_____

Remember a time you felt surprised.
What happened to make you feel surprised?

_____

_____

_____

Remember a time you felt smart.
What happened to make you feel smart?

_____

_____

_____

Remember a time you felt proud.
What happened to make you feel proud?

_____

_____

_____

Identifying cause-and-effect relationships

ANSWER KEY

THINKING SKILLS
3

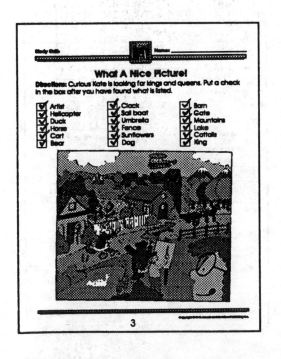

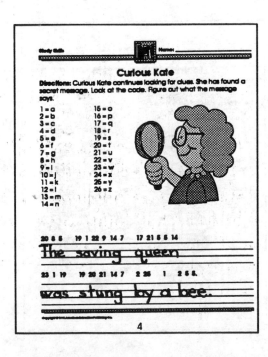

A Day At The Fair

Directions: Ann and Bill are at the fair. Read the story. Underline the 6 sentences in which Ann and/or Bill are happy.

Ann and Bill each have $5 to spend at the fair. As they walk to the fair, Ann thinks that she lost her money. She checks her pockets. Then she and Bill start looking in the grass. Finally Ann checks the pocket on her jeans again and finds her money. When Ann and Bill get to the fair they look at all the rides. They decide to go on a roller coaster. They are quiet while they wait. They scream when they are riding the roller coaster. When the ride is done, they get off laughing. Bill is hungry. Ann says, "Let's buy ice cream cones." As they eat their ice cream they play a few games. Ann wins a big stuffed animal. Bill does not win anything. After three hours at the fair Ann and Bill are tired. As they walk home they talk about their exciting day.

5

Dictionary Entries

Directions: Words in a dictionary are called entries. Some entries have more than one meaning. Dictionaries number each meaning. Look at the word and its meanings. Then answer the questions.

Fan — 1. An instrument shaped in a half-circle and waved by hand. 2. An instrument with rotating blades that stirs the air. 3. To cause air to blow. 4. A person with a special interest.

1. How many meanings are listed for fan? **4**

2. Write the meaning listed that describes a baseball fan.

A person with a special interest.

3. What is the first meaning of fan listed?

An instrument waved by hand.

4. Read this sentence: She will fan herself because she is hot. What is the best meaning for fan as it is used in this sentence?

To cause air to blow.

5. Read the second meaning of fan. Now write a sentence using that kind of a fan in it.

Answers vary

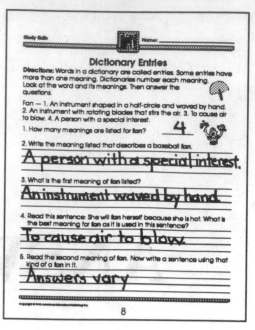

8

Looking Up Words In The Dictionary

Directions: Help Mrs. Posey find the names of her flowers in the dictionary.

Guide words are the first and last words on a dictionary page. All words on that page come between those two.

Look at the flower on the left. Circle the pair of guide words that the flower's name would be between.

1. rose — rain – refuse / **rock – rode** / (roar – ruler)

4. sunflower — slip – space / (such – swim) / some – sun

2. daisy — batt – bar / (dad – deck) / date – delight

5. violet — vase – vant / (vine – visit) / visit – voice

3. tulip — tuba – tug / (track – twin) / two – us

6. lily — lamb – late / (light – like) / light – line

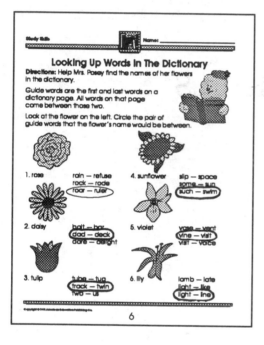

6

Using The Dictionary

Directions: Look up each word in a dictionary. Then write a sentence using it.

There are different kinds of dictionaries. Some are especially for children. Three of those are: The American Heritage Children's Dictionary, Simon and Schuster's Illustrated Young Readers' Dictionary, and Macmillan Dictionary for Children.

1. fond

sentences vary

2. pride

3. reef

4. wit

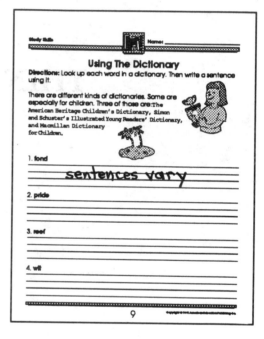

9

Learning Dictionary Skills

Directions: Mrs. Posey is ready to plant. Unscramble these gardening words. Then circle the 10 words that come between flower and glove in the dictionary. The first one is done for you.

1. lyf — (fly)
2. ridt — dirt
3. oodf — (food)
4. eeds — seed
5. truif — (fruit)
6. estfor — (forest)
7. shvelo — shovel
8. therga — (gather)
9. rgass — (grass)
10. grfo — (frog)
11. rptty — pretty
12. lufl — (full)
13. nedrag — garden
14. ateg — (gate)
15. krae — rake
16. figt — (gift)

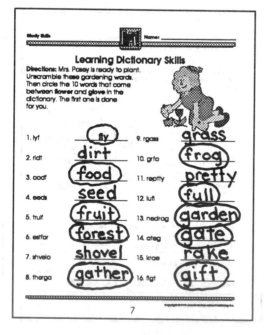

7

Review

Directions: Look at each question. Follow the instructions.

1. Read the story. Underline the 2 sentences when you think Ann is happy. Box the one sentence when you think Ann is scared. Circle the one sentence when you think Ann is sad.

Ann is glad that she and Bill are in line to go on the roller coaster. Ann has never been on such a big ride before. She is biting her lip because she is nervous. Bill says he does not want to go with her. Ann does not want to go alone. She is not happy, but she gets out of the line with Bill. Bill changes his mind. "Yes, I do want to go," he says. Ann is glad her friend will go, too.

2. Circle the words that would be between **fly** and **game** in the dictionary.

(fog) (forty) float (full) guess gate gave (gallon) (forgot) (fox)

3. Read the dictionary entry for **gauze**. Then write a sentence using **gauze** in it.

gauze — a very thin, loosely woven cloth mostly used for bandages.

sentence will vary

10

74

Page 11

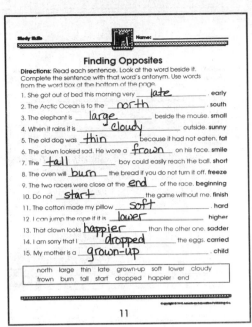

Study Skills — Name: _____

Finding Opposites

Directions: Read each sentence. Look at the word beside it. Complete the sentence with that word's antonym. Use words from the word box at the bottom of the page.

1. She got out of bed this morning very **late** . early
2. The Arctic Ocean is to the **north** . south
3. The elephant is **large** beside the mouse. small
4. When it rains it is **cloudy** outside. sunny
5. The old dog was **thin** because it had not eaten. fat
6. The clown looked sad. He wore a **frown** on his face. smile
7. The **tall** boy could easily reach the ball. short
8. The oven will **burn** the bread if you do not turn it off. freeze
9. The two racers were close at the **end** of the race. beginning
10. Do not **start** the game without me. finish
11. The cotton made my pillow **soft** . hard
12. I can jump the rope if it is **lower** . higher
13. That clown looks **happier** than the other one. sadder
14. I am sorry that I **dropped** the eggs. carried
15. My mother is a **grown-up** . child

north	large	thin	late	grown-up	soft	lower	cloudy
frown	burn	tall	start	dropped	happier	end	

11

Page 14

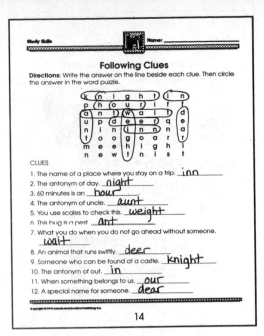

Study Skills — Name: _____

Following Clues

Directions: Write the answer on the line beside each clue. Then circle the answer in the word puzzle.

```
k n i g h t   i n
p h o u r i f
a n p d e e n   d e a
u a i o e i n   q a
m o e n g h   n r h
    n e w   n l t   i s   t
```

CLUES

1. The name of a place where you stay on a trip. **inn**
2. The antonym of day. **night**
3. 60 minutes is an **hour**
4. The antonym of uncle. **aunt**
5. You use scales to check this. **weight**
6. This bug is a pest. **ant**
7. What you do when you do not go ahead without someone. **wait**
8. An animal that runs swiftly. **deer**
9. Someone who can be found at a castle. **knight**
10. The antonym of out. **in**
11. When something belongs to us. **our**
12. A special name for someone. **dear**

14

Page 12

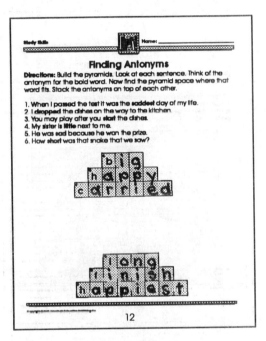

Study Skills — Name: _____

Finding Antonyms

Directions: Build the pyramids. Look at each sentence. Think of the antonym for the bold word. Now find the pyramid space where that word fits. Stack the antonyms on top of each other.

1. When I passed the test it was the **saddest** day of my life.
2. I **dropped** the dishes on the way to the kitchen.
3. You may play after you **start** the dishes.
4. My sister is **little** next to me.
5. He was **sad** because he won the prize.
6. How **short** was that snake that we saw?

```
big
happy
carried
```

```
long
finish
happiest
```

12

Page 15

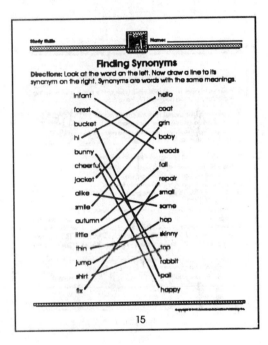

Study Skills — Name: _____

Finding Synonyms

Directions: Look at the word on the left. Now draw a line to its synonym on the right. Synonyms are words with the same meanings.

infant	hello
forest	coat
bucket	grin
hi	baby
bunny	woods
cheerful	fall
jacket	repair
alike	small
smile	same
autumn	hop
little	skinny
thin	top
jump	rabbit
shirt	pail
fix	happy

15

Page 13

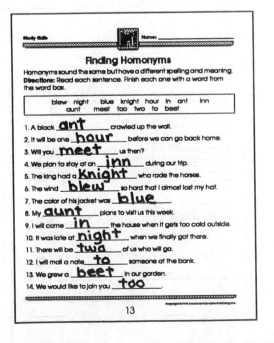

Study Skills — Name: _____

Finding Homonyms

Homonyms sound the same but have a different spelling and meaning.
Directions: Read each sentence. Finish each one with a word from the word box.

blew	night	blue	knight	hour	in	ant	inn
aunt	meet	too	two	to	beet		

1. A black **ant** crawled up the wall.
2. It will be one **hour** before we can go back home.
3. Will you **meet** us then?
4. We plan to stay at an **inn** during our trip.
5. The king had a **knight** who rode the horses.
6. The wind **blew** so hard that I almost lost my hat.
7. The color of his jacket was **blue** .
8. My **aunt** plans to visit us this week.
9. I will come **in** the house when it gets too cold outside.
10. It was late **night** when we finally got there.
11. There will be **two** of us who will go.
12. I will mail a note **to** someone at the bank.
13. We grew a **beet** in our garden.
14. We would like to join you **too**

13

Page 16

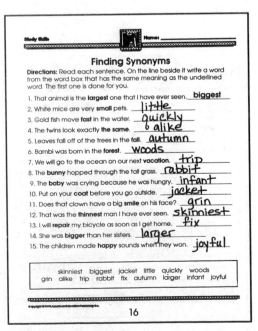

Study Skills — Name: _____

Finding Synonyms

Directions: Read each sentence. On the line beside it write a word from the word box that has the same meaning as the underlined word. The first one is done for you.

1. That animal is the **largest** one that I have ever seen. **biggest**
2. White mice are very **small** pets. **little**
3. Gold fish move **fast** in the water. **quickly**
4. The twins look exactly **the same.** **alike**
5. Leaves fall off of the trees in the **fall.** **autumn**
6. Bambi was born in the **forest.** **woods**
7. We will go to the ocean on our next **vacation.** **trip**
8. The **bunny** hopped through the tall grass. **rabbit**
9. The **baby** was crying because he was hungry. **infant**
10. Put on your **coat** before you go outside. **jacket**
11. Does that clown have a big **smile** on his face? **grin**
12. That was the **thinnest** man I have ever seen. **skinniest**
13. I will **repair** my bicycle as soon as I get home. **fix**
14. She was **bigger** than her sisters. **larger**
15. The children made **happy** sounds when they won. **joyful**

skinniest	biggest	jacket	little	quickly	woods
grin	alike	trip	rabbit	fix	autumn	larger	infant	joyful

16

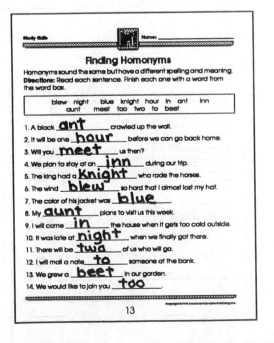

75

Kate Is Looking For Synonyms

Directions: Curious Kate is looking for synonyms. Look at the clues. Fill in the puzzle with a synonym for each clue.

Across
1. us
2. hop
3. skinny
4. jacket
5. top

Down
1. forest
2. coat
3. shirt
4. sleepy
5. kind

tired
jacket
top
woods
thin
we
shirt
coat
jump
nice

17

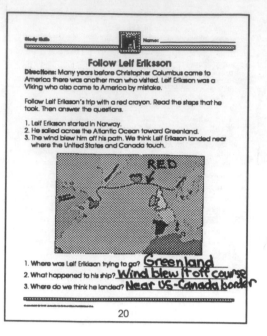

Follow Leif Eriksson

Directions: Many years before Christopher Columbus came to America there was another man who visited. Leif Eriksson was a Viking who also came to America by mistake.

Follow Leif Eriksson's trip with a red crayon. Read the steps that he took. Then answer the questions.

1. Leif Eriksson started in Norway.
2. He sailed across the Atlantic Ocean toward Greenland.
3. The wind blew him off his path. We think Leif Eriksson landed near where the United States and Canada touch.

1. Where was Leif Eriksson trying to go? **Greenland**
2. What happened to his ship? **Wind blew it off course**
3. Where do we think he landed? **Near US-Canada border**

20

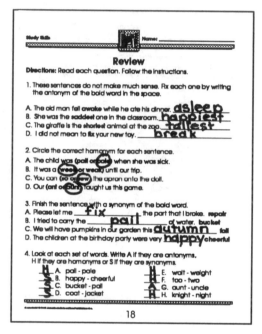

Review

Directions: Read each question. Follow the instructions.

1. These sentences do not make much sense. Fix each one by writing the antonym of the bold word in the space.
A. The old man fell awake while he ate his dinner. **asleep**
B. She was the saddest one in the classroom. **happiest**
C. The giraffe is the shortest animal at the zoo. **tallest**
D. I did not mean to fix your new toy. **break**

2. Circle the correct homonym for each sentence.
A. The child was (pail or pale) when she was sick.
B. It was a (week or weak) until our trip.
C. You can (so or sew) the apron onto the doll.
D. Our (ant or aunt) taught us this game.

3. Finish the sentence with a synonym of the bold word.
A. Please let me **fix** the part that I broke. repair
B. I tried to carry the **pail** of water. bucket
C. We will have pumpkins in our garden this **autumn**. fall
D. The children at the birthday party were very **happy**. cheerful

4. Look at each set of words. Write A if they are antonyms, H if they are homonyms or S if they are synonyms.
  H A. pail - pale   H E. wait - weight
  S B. happy - cheerful H F. too - two
  S C. bucket - pail   A G. aunt - uncle
  S D. coat - jacket   H H. knight - night

18

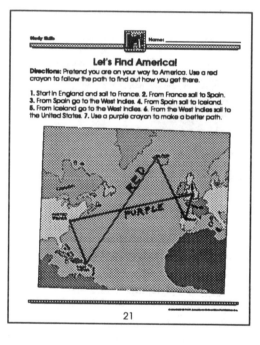

Let's Find America!

Directions: Pretend you are on your way to America. Use a red crayon to follow the path to find out how you get there.

1. Start in England and sail to France. 2. From France sail to Spain. 3. From Spain go to the West Indies. 4. From Spain sail to Iceland. 5. From Iceland go to the West Indies. 6. From the West Indies sail to the United States. 7. Use a purple crayon to make a better path.

21

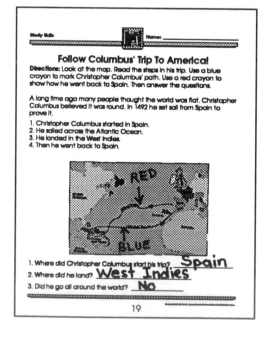

Follow Columbus' Trip To America!

Directions: Look at the map. Read the steps in his trip. Use a blue crayon to mark Christopher Columbus' path. Use a red crayon to show how he went back to Spain. Then answer the questions.

A long time ago many people thought the world was flat. Christopher Columbus believed it was round. In 1492 he set sail from Spain to prove it.

1. Christopher Columbus started in Spain.
2. He sailed across the Atlantic Ocean.
3. He landed in the West Indies.
4. Then he went back to Spain.

1. Where did Christopher Columbus start his trip? **Spain**
2. Where did he land? **West Indies**
3. Did he go all around the world? **No**

19

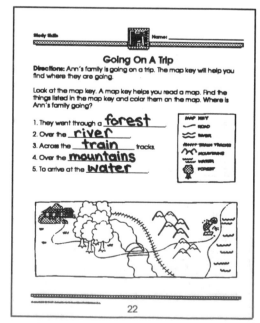

Going On A Trip

Directions: Ann's family is going on a trip. The map key will help you find where they are going.

Look at the map key. A map key helps you read a map. Find the things listed in the map key and color them on the map. Where is Ann's family going?

1. They went through a **forest**
2. Over the **river**
3. Across the **train** tracks.
4. Over the **mountains**
5. To arrive at the **water**

MAP KEY
— ROAD
~ RIVER
+++ TRAIN TRACKS
^ MOUNTAINS
≈ WATER
♣ FOREST

22

Learning Map Skills

Directions: Look at the map key. Now draw a map of your neighborhood. Use the map key to help you find things to put on your map.

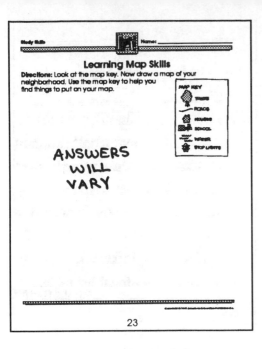

ANSWERS
WILL
VARY

23

How Far Is It?

Directions: Miles show how far away one place is from another. Look at the map scale. It shows you that one inch equals one mile. Now use the map scale to find out how far Ann's home is from other places.

Map Scale
1 inch = 1 mile

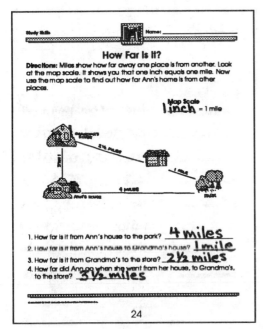

1. How far is it from Ann's house to the park? **4 miles**
2. How far is it from Ann's house to Grandma's house? **1 mile**
3. How far is it from Grandma's to the store? **2½ miles**
4. How far did Ann go when she went from her house, to Grandma's, to the store? **3½ miles**

24

Ann And Bill At The Playground

Directions: Ann and Bill are at the playground. Look at the map scale. Use a ruler to measure the map so you can answer the questions.

Map Scale
1 inch = 1 foot

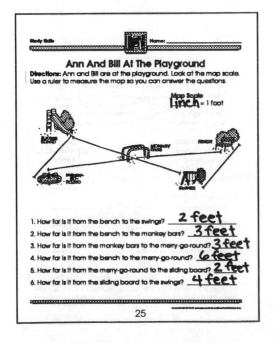

1. How far is it from the bench to the swings? **2 feet**
2. How far is it from the bench to the monkey bars? **3 feet**
3. How far is it from the monkey bars to the merry-go-round? **3 feet**
4. How far is it from the bench to the merry-go-round? **6 feet**
5. How far is it from the merry-go-round to the sliding board? **2 feet**
6. How far is it from the sliding board to the swings? **4 feet**

25

Review

Directions: Curious Kate knows that there is a treasure buried in the park. Use your new map skills to make her path. Answer the questions.

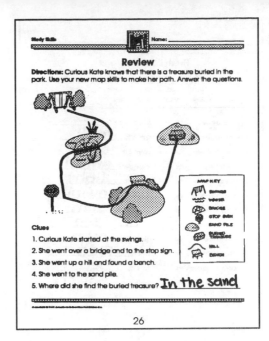

Clues

1. Curious Kate started at the swings.
2. She went over a bridge and to the stop sign.
3. She went up a hill and found a bench.
4. She went to the sand pile.
5. Where did she find the buried treasure? **In the sand**

26

Comparing Similarities

Directions: Analogies are made when things are compared to each other. Look at the example. Think about how each pair is related. Then finish the other analogies on this page.

EXAMPLE

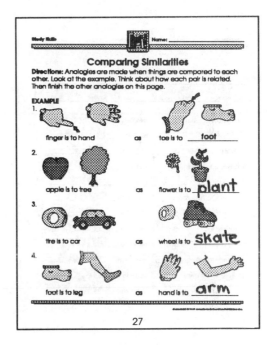

1. finger is to hand   as   toe is to **foot**

2. apple is to tree   as   flower is to **plant**

3. tire is to car   as   wheel is to **skate**

4. foot is to leg   as   hand is to **arm**

27

Making Analogies

Directions: Look at each analogy. Choose a word from the word box to finish it.

| week | bottom | month | tiny |
| sentence | lake | out | eye |

1. up is to down   as   in is to **out**
2. minute is to hour   as   day is to **week**
3. month is to year   as   week is to **month**
4. over is to under   as   top is to **bottom**
5. big is to little   as   giant is to **tiny**
6. sound is to ear   as   sight is to **eye**
7. page is to book   as   word is to **sentence**
8. wood is to tree   as   water is to **lake**

28

77

Finish Each Analogy

Directions: Finish each analogy with a word from the word box.

dog	fish	cup	left	south	cat
light	bear	small	arm	zoo	evening

1. hive is to bee as dog house is to __dog__
2. up is to down as right is to __left__
3. lamb is to sheep as kitten is to __cat__
4. big is to little as large is to __small__
5. black is to white as dark is to __light__
6. day is to night as morning is to __evening__
7. knee is to leg as elbow is to __arm__
8. chicken is to farm as monkey is to __zoo__
9. fork is to spoon as glass is to __cup__
10. wing is to bird as fin is to __fish__
11. feather is to duck as fur is to __bear__
12. east is to west as north is to __south__

29

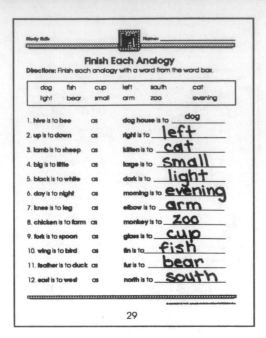

Sequencing

Directions: Look at each group of words. The sequence is mixed up. Unscramble the sequence so that it is from least to most.

EXAMPLE:
minute, second, hour → second, minutes, hour

1. least, most, more → least, more, most
2. full, empty, half-full → empty, half-full, full
3. month, day, year → day, month, year
4. baseball, golf ball, soccer ball → golf ball, baseball, soccer ball
5. penny, dollar, quarter → penny, quarter, dollar
6. $4.12, $3.18, $3.22 → $3.18, $3.22, $4.12
7. boy, man, infant → infant, boy, man
8. mother, daughter, grandmother → daughter, mother, grandmother

32

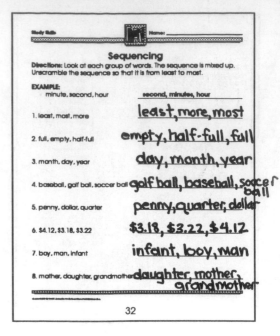

Finish Each Analogy

Directions: Finish the analogy with a word from the word box.

finish	less	pony	oven	finger	big
week	hour	cat	weak	under	little

1. second is to minute as minute is to __hour__
2. fast is to slow as big is to __little__
3. child is to mother as kitten is to __cat__
4. puppy is to kitten as calf is to __pony__
5. less is to more as little is to __big__
6. freeze is to freezer as bake is to __oven__
7. late is to early as more is to __less__
8. first is to last as start is to __finish__
9. in is to out as over is to __under__
10. hard is to soft as strong is to __weak__
11. earring is to ear as ring is to __finger__
12. hour is to day as day is to __week__

30

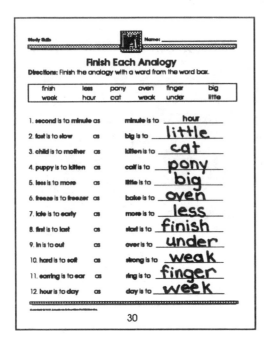

Sequencing

Directions: Look at each group of words. The sequence is mixed. Unscramble the sequence so that it is from largest to smallest.

1. small, medium, large → large, medium, small
2. toddler, baby, child → child, toddler, baby
3. year, minute, day → year, day, minute
4. $5.50, $6.25, $5.75 → $6.25, $5.75, $5.50
5. thirty, ten, twenty → thirty, twenty, ten
6. gallon, quart, pint → gallon, quart, pint
7. half, quarter, whole → whole, half, quarter
8. most, least, same → most, same, least

33

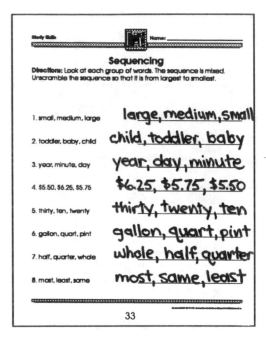

Putting Things In Order

Directions: Look at each question. The two words there suggest an order called a sequence. Choose a word from the word box to finish the sequence. Be careful. There are more words in the word box than you need. The first one is done for you.

below	three	fifteen	December	twenty	under
after	go	third	hour	March	yard

1. January, February, __March__
2. before, during, __after__
3. over, on, __under__
4. come, stay, __go__
5. second, minute, __hour__
6. first, second, __third__
7. five, ten, __fifteen__
8. inch, foot, __yard__

31

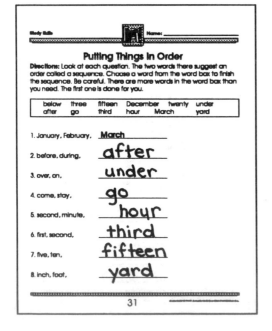

Review

Directions: Read each question. Follow the instructions.

1. Match the analogy on the left with the similar one on the right.
   finger is to hand ——— east is to west
   hard is to soft ——— toe is to foot
   left is to right ——— over is to under
   top is to bottom ——— strong is to weak

2. Finish each analogy.
   minute is to hour as day is to __week__
   up is to down as high is to __low__
   black is to white as night is to __day__
   good is to bad as right is to __wrong__

3. Complete each sequence.
   April, May, __June__
   first, second, __third__
   boy, father, __grandfather__
   yesterday, today, __tomorrow__

4. Unscramble the sequences. The order should be smallest to largest.
   large, small, medium → small, medium, large
   middle, last, first → first, middle, last
   empty, full, half-full → empty, half-full, full
   hour, second, minute → second, minute, hour

34

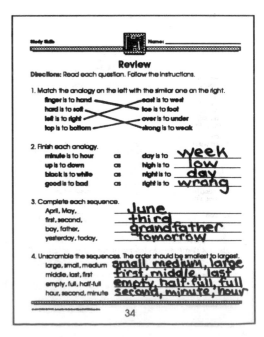

Classifying

Directions: Look at the words in the word box. Each word can be grouped with a season. Fill in the pyramids for each season with a word from the word box.

July 4	hot	football	bike rides	windy	leaves
kite	froze	sled ride	swimming	Thanksgiving	
snowman	bunnies	ice	jack-o-lantern	baseball	

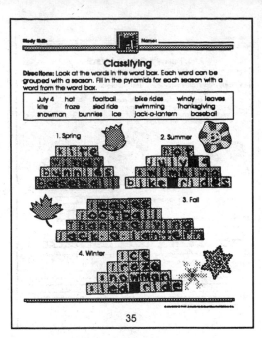

1. Spring
kite
swimming
bunnies
bike rides

2. Summer
July 4
swimming
baseball
bike rides

3. Fall
leaves
football
thanksgiving
jack-o-lantern

4. Winter
ice
froze
snowman
sled ride

35

Help Mrs. Posey

Directions: Mrs. Posey is sorting out the names of birds from the names of the trees and the flowers. Move each word from the word box to its right place. Put 4 words in each box.

robin	elm
buckeye	willow
sunflower	bluejay
canary	oak
rose	wren
tulip	morning glory

Birds
robin
bluejay
wren
canary

Trees
elm
buckeye
willow
oak

Flowers
sunflower
rose
tulip
morning glory

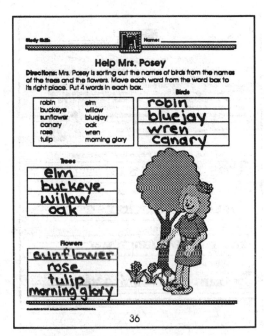

36

Animal Stories

Directions: Read each animal story. Then look at the fun facts. Beside each fact put an H for horse, P for panda or D for Dog.

Horses
Horses are fun to ride. You can ride them in the woods or in fields. Horses usually have pretty names. Sometimes, if they are golden, they are called Amber. When it is hot they swish their tails. That keeps the flies away from them.

Pandas
Pandas are from China. They like to climb trees. They scratch bark to write messages to their friends in the trees. When Pandas get hungry, they gnaw on bamboo shoots!

Dogs
Dogs are good pets. A lot of times people call them names like Spot or Fido. Sometimes they are named after their looks. For example, a brown dog is sometimes named Brownie. Some people have special, small doors for their dogs to use.

Fun Facts

D 1. My name is often Spot or Fido.
P 2. I am from China.
D 3. Snoopy is my friend.
H 4. I like to carry people into the fields.
P 5. My favorite food is bamboo.
H 6. Flies bother me when I am hot.
H 7. Amber is often my name when I am golden.
P 8. I leave messages for my friends by scratching bark.
D 9. Sometimes I have my own special door on a house.

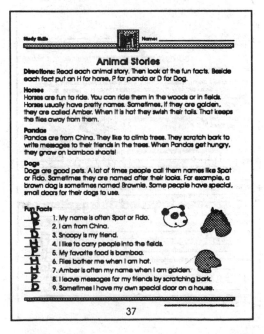

37

People Of Wackyville

Directions: Compare the people of Wackyville to each other. Read the first sentence. Think about it. Then read the second sentence. Answer the question. The first one is done for you.

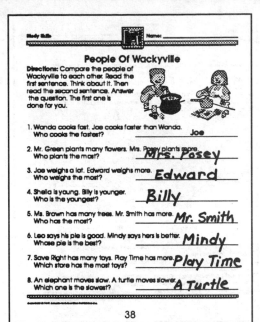

1. Wanda cooks fast. Joe cooks faster than Wanda. Who cooks the fastest? Joe

2. Mr. Green plants many flowers. Mrs. Posey plants more. Who plants the most? Mrs. Posey

3. Joe weighs a lot. Edward weighs more. Who weighs the most? Edward

4. Sheila is young. Billy is younger. Who is the youngest? Billy

5. Ms. Brown has many trees. Mr. Smith has more. Who has the most? Mr. Smith

6. Leo says his pie is good. Mindy says hers is better. Whose pie is the best? Mindy

7. Save Right has many toys. Play Time has more. Which store has the most toys? Play Time

8. An elephant moves slow. A turtle moves slower. Which one is the slowest? A Turtle

38

Making Deductions

Directions: Carefully read each sentence. Answer the question.

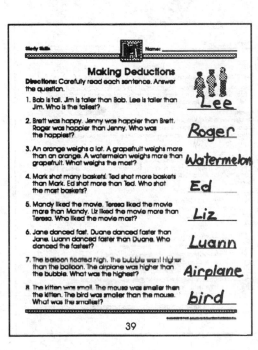

1. Bob is tall. Jim is taller than Bob. Lee is taller than Jim. Who is the tallest? Lee

2. Brett was happy. Jenny was happier than Brett. Roger was happier than Jenny. Who was the happiest? Roger

3. An orange weighs a lot. A grapefruit weighs more than an orange. A watermelon weighs more than grapefruit. What weighs the most? Watermelon

4. Mark shot many baskets. Ted shot more baskets than Mark. Ed shot more than Ted. Who shot the most baskets? Ed

5. Mandy liked the movie. Teresa liked the movie more than Mandy. Liz liked the movie more than Teresa. Who liked the movie most? Liz

6. Jane danced fast. Duane danced faster than Jane. Luann danced faster than Duane. Who danced the fastest? Luann

7. The balloon floated high. The bubble went higher than the balloon. The airplane was higher than the bubble. What was the highest? Airplane

8. The kitten was small. The mouse was smaller than the kitten. The bird was smaller than the mouse. What was the smallest? bird

39

Hunting For Holly

Directions: Ann's pet dog, Holly, has disappeared. Help Ann and her friends find Holly.

Look at the picture of Ann's house. Then read the clues. Write the person's name on the line in the room where they were.

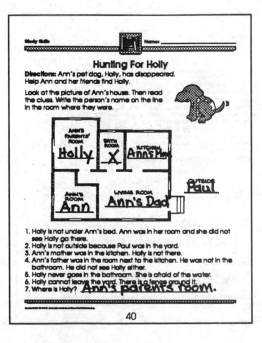

1. Holly is not under Ann's bed. Ann was in her room and she did not see Holly go there.
2. Holly is not outside because Paul was in the yard.
3. Ann's mother was in the kitchen. Holly is not there.
4. Ann's father was in the room next to the kitchen. He was not in the bathroom. He did not see Holly either.
5. Holly never goes in the bathroom. She is afraid of the water.
6. Holly cannot leave the yard. There is a fence around it.
7. Where is Holly? Ann's parents room.

40

79

The Winning Hit

Directions: Read the story. Use the softball diamond to find out who made the winning hit. Write the players' names on the line where they were.

Ann and her friends are playing a game of softball. The score is tied. The luck of the next batter will decide who wins the game. Ann's team includes Bill, John, Jane, Mary and Martha.

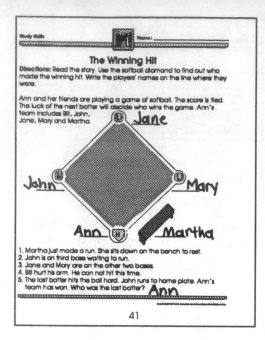

Jane

John   Mary

Ann   Martha

1. Martha just made a run. She sits down on the bench to rest.
2. John is on third base waiting to run.
3. Jane and Mary are on the other two bases.
4. Bill hurt his arm. He can not hit this time.
5. The last batter hits the ball hard. John runs to home plate. Ann's team has won. Who was the last batter? **Ann**

41

Mrs. Posey's Colorful Yard!

Directions: Read the story. Answer the questions.

Mrs. Posey plants roses everywhere. She plants yellow roses near her front porch. She plants red roses near the back door. There are also pink roses and white roses in her yard. Every time the mailman comes to her house, he sneezes. "You should not plant so many flowers," he tells Mrs. Posey. Mrs. Posey just smiles.

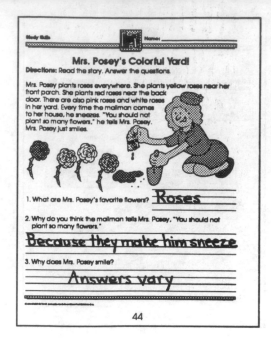

1. What are Mrs. Posey's favorite flowers? **Roses**

2. Why do you think the mailman tells Mrs. Posey, "You should not plant so many flowers."

Because they make him sneeze

3. Why does Mrs. Posey smile?

Answers vary

44

Review

Directions: Look at each question. Follow the instructions.

1. Read each paragraph. Then look at the Fun Facts. Decide if each fact describes potato chips, a hot dog or a popsicle. Put C for potato chips, H for hot dog or P for popsicle.

Potato Chips
Once upon a time a man was eating french fries. He thought they were too soggy. When he sent them back to the chef, the chef cut some potatos very thin and fried them. These were the first potato chips!

Hot Dogs
Hot dogs have not always been called hot dogs. A long time ago people only called them frankfurters. But an artist who was at a baseball game drew a picture of frankfurter and put it on a bun. He made the frankfurter look like a dog! Then he wrote "hot dog" under his picture!

Popsicles
One cold night in 1905 a man named Frank Epperson left a glass of lemonade on a windowsill. It had a stirring stick in it. The lemonade froze and the first popsicle was born. But the popsicle was called an Epsicle at first.

H They used to be called frankfurters.
C A chef sliced them thin and fried them.
P The first one was made of frozen lemonade.
H The first picture of one of these was drawn at a baseball game.
P It was first called the Epsicle after Frank Epperson who invented it.
C A customer thought his french fries were too soggy.
H The person who named them thought they looked like dogs.
P It was invented in 1905 with a glass and a stick.

42

Mrs. Posey Gets Hurt

Directions: Read about Mrs. Posey again. Then answer the questions.

Mrs. Posey is working in her rose garden. She is trimming the branches so that the plants will grow better. Mrs. Posey is careful because rose bushes have thorns on them. "Hello, Mrs. Posey," calls Ann as she rides her bicycle down the street. "Hi, Ann," she calls back. Then she yells, "Ouch." She runs inside the house and stays there for a few minutes. When Mrs. Posey comes outside she has a bandage on one finger.

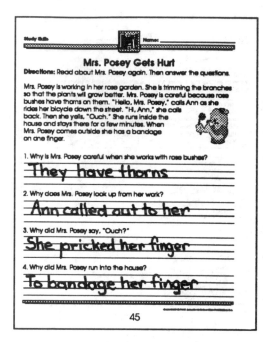

1. Why is Mrs. Posey careful when she works with rose bushes?

They have thorns

2. Why does Mrs. Posey look up from her work?

Ann called out to her

3. Why did Mrs. Posey say, "Ouch?"

She pricked her finger

4. Why did Mrs. Posey run into the house?

To bandage her finger

45

The Jitterbug

Directions: Read about the jitterbug. Then answer the questions.

The music is playing loudly. Paul and Mary are facing each other. They hold hands. They are going to do something called the jitterbug. Paul starts bouncing back and forth, first on one foot, then on the other. Mary starts doing the same thing. They are "keeping time" to the music's beat. Then they start moving around a lot. Mary ducks under Paul's arm. They are laughing because they are having fun.

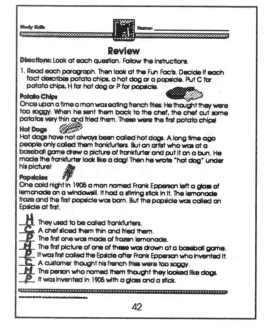

1. What are Paul and Mary doing? **Dancing**

2. Why are they bouncing back and forth, first on one foot then on the other?

To keep time with the music

3. Why are Paul and Mary laughing?

Dancing the jitterbug is fun

43

Something Is Hiding!

Directions: Read about cocoons. Then answer the questions.

Some people do not like caterpillars. They look like fuzzy worms. They have many legs and they creep and crawl in trees and leaves. But a caterpillar is really the beginning of something else. It eats leaves for many days. After it is very big it spins a cocoon. It stays inside for a few months. When the cocoon opens something else is inside. It is very beautiful. It flies away.

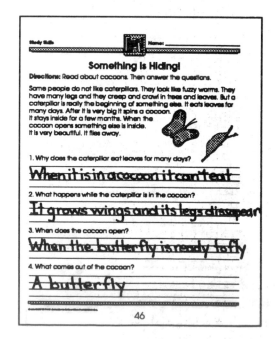

1. Why does the caterpillar eat leaves for many days?

When it is in a cocoon it can't eat

2. What happens while the caterpillar is in the cocoon?

It grows wings and its legs disappear

3. When does the cocoon open?

When the butterfly is ready to fly

4. What comes out of the cocoon?

A butterfly

46

Page 47:

Butterflies Protect Themselves!

Directions: Read about butterflies. Then answer the questions.

Butterflies are many different colors. They have different designs on them, too. These colors and designs help them. When some butterflies are resting they look like leaves. Animals cannot see them. Other butterflies smell funny. Animals do not like the smell.

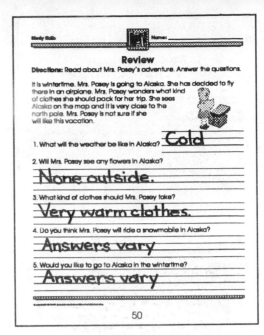

1. How do the different colors and designs help protect butterflies?

To help them hide from animals

2. What do they need protection from?

Animals that may eat them

3. Why do some butterflies look like leaves?

So they can hide in trees and bushes

4. Why do some butterflies smell funny?

To keep animals from eating them

47

Page 50:

Review

Directions: Read about Mrs. Posey's adventure. Answer the questions.

It is wintertime. Mrs. Posey is going to Alaska. She has decided to fly there in an airplane. Mrs. Posey wonders what kind of clothes she should pack for her trip. She sees Alaska on the map and it is very close to the north pole. Mrs. Posey is not sure if she will like this vacation.

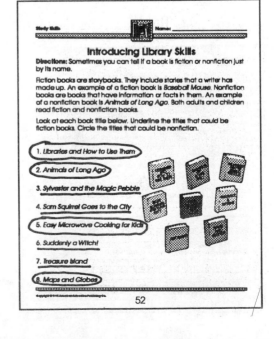

1. What will the weather be like in Alaska? Cold

2. Will Mrs. Posey see any flowers in Alaska?

None outside.

3. What kind of clothes should Mrs. Posey take?

Very warm clothes.

4. Do you think Mrs. Posey will ride a snowmobile in Alaska?

Answers vary

5. Would you like to go to Alaska in the wintertime?

Answers vary

50

Page 48:

Eskimos Of Long Ago

Directions: Read about Eskimos. Then answer the questions.

Eskimos live in Alaska. A long time ago Eskimos lived in houses made of snow, dirt or animal skins. They moved around from place to place a lot. The Eskimos hunted and fished. Often they ate raw meat because they had no way to cook it. When they ate it raw, they liked it dried or frozen. Eskimos used animal skin for their clothes. They used fat from whales, seals and other animals to heat their houses.

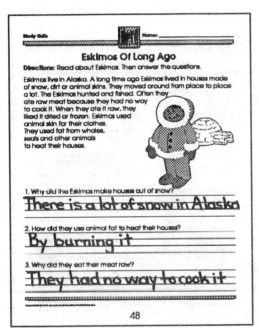

1. Why did the Eskimos make houses out of snow?

There is a lot of snow in Alaska

2. How did they use animal fat to heat their houses?

By burning it

3. Why did they eat their meat raw?

They had no way to cook it

48

Page 51:

Learning How To Use The Library

Directions: A library is a place that has many books. People can borrow the books and read them. Then they take them back to the library.

Most libraries have two sections. One is for adults' books and one is for children's books. A librarian is there to help people find books.

Read the title of each library book. On the line under each title write A if you think it is an adult's book or C if you think it is a children's book.

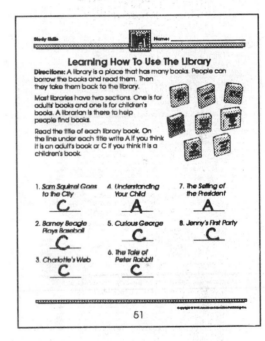

1. Sam Squirrel Goes to the City — C

2. Barney Beagle Plays Baseball — C

3. Charlotte's Web — C

4. Understanding Your Child — A

5. Curious George — C

6. The Tale of Peter Rabbit — C

7. The Setting of the President — A

8. Jenny's First Party — C

51

Page 49:

Eskimos Have Changed!

Directions: Read about today's Eskimos. Then answer the questions.

Today, many Eskimos stay in villages instead of always moving around. They work in jobs, instead of hunting and fishing. Eskimo children go to school, too. Their houses are heated from oil out of the ground, instead of animal oil. Many Eskimos use snowmobiles instead of dogs and sleds. In the winter they wear coats that are very warm.

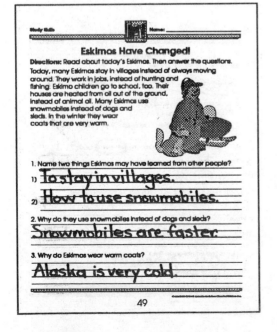

1. Name two things Eskimos may have learned from other people?

1) To stay in villages.

2) How to use snowmobiles.

2. Why do they use snowmobiles instead of dogs and sleds?

Snowmobiles are faster.

3. Why do Eskimos wear warm coats?

Alaska is very cold.

49

Page 52:

Introducing Library Skills

Directions: Sometimes you can tell if a book is fiction or nonfiction just by its name.

Fiction books are storybooks. They include stories that a writer has made up. An example of a fiction book is *Baseball Mouse*. Nonfiction books are books that have information or facts in them. An example of a nonfiction book is *Animals of Long Ago*. Both adults and children read fiction and nonfiction books.

Look at each book title below. Underline the titles that could be fiction books. Circle the titles that could be nonfiction.

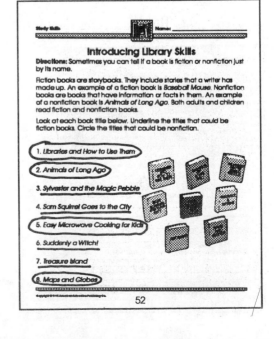

1. Libraries and How to Use Them
2. Animals of Long Ago
3. Sylvester and the Magic Pebble
4. Sam Squirrel Goes to the City
5. Easy Microwave Cooking for Kids
6. Suddenly a Witch!
7. Treasure Island
8. Maps and Globes

52

81

Finding Books In A Library

Directions: Fiction books in a library are filed in ABC order using the author's last name.

Example: Jack Ezra Keats would be Keats, Jack Ezra.

Nonfiction books are grouped by subjects. For example, all books about snakes are grouped together and all books about outer space are grouped together.

Practice filing books in ABC order. Here is a list of author's names. On the line beside the name put the number of where that book would come in ABC order.

7 Rand, Ann and Paul
2 Burton, Virginia Lee
4 Keats, Ezra Jack
8 Rey, H. A.
3 Irving, Washington
5 Lionni, Leo
6 Potter, Beatrix
1 Blume, Judy

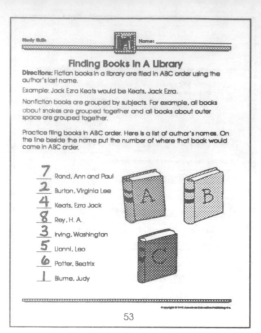

Encyclopedias And Dictionaries

Directions: Reference books are books that tell you basic facts. Dictionaries and encyclopedias are reference books. You usually are not allowed to take reference books out of the library.

Dictionaries tell you about words. Encyclopedias give you other information, such as when the president was born, what the Civil War was, and where Eskimos live. Encyclopedias usually come in sets of more than 20 books. Information is listed in ABC order, just like words are listed in the dictionary.

There are other kinds of reference books, too. These can include books of maps, called atlases. Reference books are hardly ever read cover to cover.

Read each fact. Draw a line from the fact to the book that you would use to find it. Is it about a dictionary or is it about an encyclopedia? The first one is done for you.

1. I would have the definition of divide in me.
2. I would tell you when George Washington was born.
3. I would give you the correct spelling for many words.
4. I would tell you where Indians live.
5. I would tell you the names of many butterflies.
6. I would tell you what modern means.
7. I would give you the history of dinosaurs.
8. If you have to write a paper about Eskimos, I could help you.

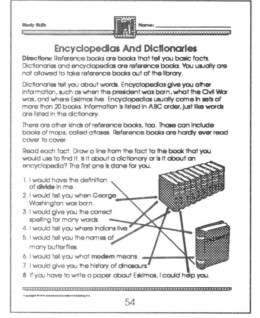

Periodicals

Directions: Learn about magazines and newspapers.

Magazines and newspapers are called periodicals. Libraries usually have some of them, too.

There are many kinds of magazines. Some tell you about children. Others have recipes in them. Some magazines have information about the world in them. There is even a magazine about Nintendo!

Almost every city and town has a newspaper. Newspapers can come out every day or every week or every month. Newspapers tell you what is happening in your town and in the world. They have sections about sports and about clothes. They give you a lot of information.

Look at each question. Follow the instructions.

1. Find a magazine that you would like to look through. What is its name?

Answer varies

List the names of three stories in the magazine.
1. **Answers vary**
2. _____
3. _____

2. Now look at a newspaper. What is its name?

Answer varies

The titles of newspaper stories are called headlines. What are some of the headlines in your newspaper?
1. **Answers vary**
2. _____

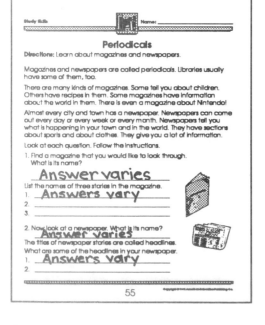

Paul And Mary Go To The Library

Directions: Paul and Mary are going to the library to get some facts about the moon. Where should they look while they are there?

Answer the questions to help Paul and Mary find out where they can get information about the moon at the library.

1. Should they look in the children's section or in the adults' section? — **Either**

2. Should they look for a fiction book or a nonfiction book? — **nonfiction**

3. Who at the library can help them? — **Librarian**

4. What reference book should they look in? — **Encyclopedia**

5. Where else can they look for information that may have been in the news? — **Newspapers Magazines**

6. What word would they look up in the encyclopedia to get the information that they need? — **Moon**

Puzzling Out Library Terms

Directions: Read each clue. Use some of the words from the word box to finish the crossword puzzle.

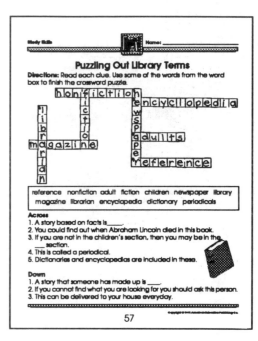

reference nonfiction adult fiction children newspaper library magazine librarian encyclopedia dictionary periodicals

Across
1. A story based on facts is____.
2. You could find out when Abraham Lincoln died in this book.
3. If you are not in the children's section, then you may be in the ____ section.
4. This is called a periodical.
5. Dictionaries and encyclopedias are included in these.

Down
1. A story that someone has made up is ____.
2. If you cannot find what you are looking for you should ask this person.
3. This can be delivered to your house everyday.

Review

Directions: Circle each answer.

1. A book containing only facts about outer space is a (fiction or (nonfiction)) book.

2. Books are sometimes listed in ((ABC) or 123) order according to their authors' names.

3. A book with the title, *The Ghost of Windy Hill*, is probably ((fiction) or nonfiction).

4. An encyclopedia is a (periodical or (reference)) book.

5. Newspapers and magazines are called (references or (periodicals)).

6. (True or (False)) I can keep books that I get from the library forever.

7. List three things that you can find in an encyclopedia.
1) **Answers vary**
2) _____
3) _____

8. List these authors in ABC order the way they would appear in the library: H.A. Rey, Lucy Ozone and Margaret Ott.
(Hint: Last names come first.)
1) **Ott, Margaret**
2) **Ozone, Lucy**
3) **Rey, H. A.**

Our President, The Inventor!

Directions: Read the story about Thomas Jefferson. Answer the questions.

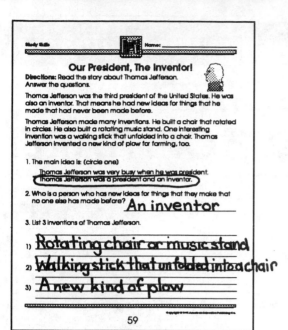

Thomas Jefferson was the third president of the United States. He was also an inventor. That means he had new ideas for things that he made that had never been made before.

Thomas Jefferson made many inventions. He built a chair that rotated in circles. He also built a rotating music stand. One interesting invention was a walking stick that unfolded into a chair. Thomas Jefferson invented a new kind of plow for farming, too.

1. The main idea is: (circle one)
   Thomas Jefferson was very busy when he was president.
   (Thomas Jefferson was a president and an inventor.)

2. Who is a person who has new ideas for things that they make that no one else has made before? **An inventor**

3. List 3 inventions of Thomas Jefferson.

1) **Rotating chair or music stand**
2) **Walking stick that unfolded into a chair**
3) **A new kind of plow**

59

Inventing The Bicycle!

Directions: Read the story about the bicycle. Then answer the questions.

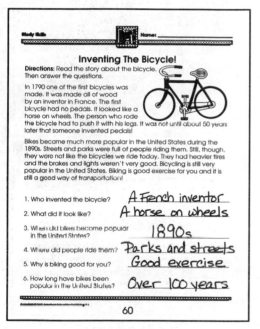

In 1790 one of the first bicycles was made. It was made all of wood by an inventor in France. The first bicycle had no pedals. It looked like a horse on wheels. The person who rode the bicycle had to push it with his legs. It was not until about 50 years later that someone invented pedals!

Bikes became much more popular in the United States during the 1890s. Streets and parks were full of people riding them. Still, though, they were not like the bicycles we ride today. They had heavier tires and the brakes and lights weren't very good. Bicycling is still very popular in the United States. Biking is good exercise for you and it is still a good way of transportation!

1. Who invented the bicycle? **A French inventor**
2. What did it look like? **A horse on wheels**
3. When did bikes become popular in the United States? **1890s**
4. Where did people ride them? **Parks and streets**
5. Why is biking good for you? **Good exercise**
6. How long have bikes been popular in the United States? **Over 100 years**

60

Discovering Chewing Gum!

Directions: Read about chewing gum. Then answer the questions.

Thomas Adams was an inventor in the United States. In 1870 he was looking for something that could replace rubber. He was working with chicle ("chick-ul") that comes from a certain kind of tree in Mexico. Years ago Mexicans chewed chicle.

Thomas Adams decided to try it! He liked it so much he started selling it. About 20 years later he owned a big factory that made chewing gum.

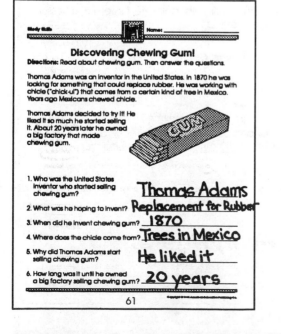

1. Who was the United States inventor who started selling chewing gum? **Thomas Adams**
2. What was he hoping to invent? **Replacement for Rubber**
3. When did he invent chewing gum? **1870**
4. Where does the chicle come from? **Trees in Mexico**
5. Why did Thomas Adams start selling chewing gum? **He liked it**
6. How long was it until he owned a big factory selling chewing gum? **20 years**

61

The Peaceful Pueblos

Directions: Read about the Pueblo Indians. Answer the questions.

The Pueblo ("Pooh-eb-low") Indians live in the southwest United States in New Mexico and Arizona. They have lived there for hundreds of years. The Pueblo Indians have always been peaceful Indians. They never started wars. They only fought if they were attacked first.

The Pueblo Indians loved to dance. Even their dances were peaceful. They danced when they asked the gods for rain or sunshine. They danced for other reasons, too. Sometimes the Pueblos wore masks when they danced.

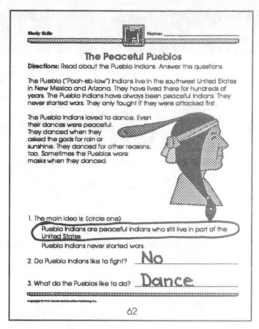

1. The main idea is: (circle one)
   (Pueblo Indians are peaceful Indians who still live in part of the United States.)
   Pueblo Indians never started wars.

2. Do Pueblo Indians like to fight? **No**

3. What do the Pueblos like to do? **Dance**

62

Homes Made Of Clay!

Directions: Read about adobe houses. Then answer the questions.

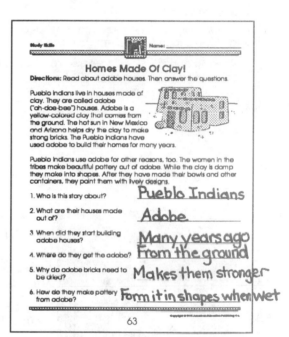

Pueblo Indians live in houses made of clay. They are called adobe ("ah-doe-bee") houses. Adobe is a yellow-colored clay that comes from the ground. The hot sun in New Mexico and Arizona helps dry the clay to make strong bricks. The Pueblo Indians have used adobe to build their homes for many years.

Pueblo Indians use adobe for other reasons, too. The women in the tribes make beautiful pottery out of adobe. While the clay is damp they make into shapes. After they have made their bowls and other containers, they paint them with lively designs.

1. Who is this story about? **Pueblo Indians**
2. What are their houses made out of? **Adobe**
3. When did they start building adobe houses? **Many years ago**
4. Where do they get the adobe? **From the ground**
5. Why do adobe bricks need to be dried? **Makes them stronger**
6. How do they make pottery from adobe? **Form it in shapes when wet**

63

Review

Directions: Read the story about George Washington. Then answer the questions.

George Washington was the first president. An old story said that he was very honest. It said that when he was six years old he cut down a cherry tree on the farm where he lived. The story said Washington could not lie about it. He told his dad he cut down the tree. But George Washington did not chop down a cherry tree. People have found out that this story was made up by someone else. They say a man named Parson Weems wrote one of the first books about George Washington. He liked Washington so much that he made up that story.

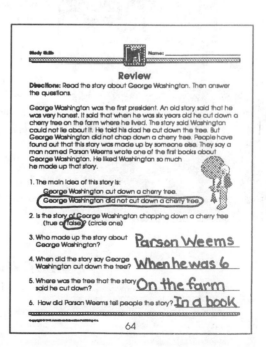

1. The main idea of this story is:
   George Washington cut down a cherry tree.
   (George Washington did not cut down a cherry tree.)

2. Is the story of George Washington chopping down a cherry tree (true or false)? (circle one)

3. Who made up the story about George Washington? **Parson Weems**
4. When did the story say George Washington cut down the tree? **When he was 6**
5. Where was the tree that the story said he cut down? **On the farm**
6. How did Parson Weems tell people the story? **In a book**

64

83

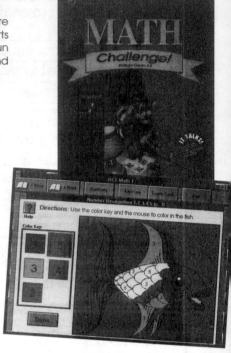

OVERVIEW

ENRICHMENT READING is designed to provide children with practice in reading and to increase students' reading abilities. The program consists of six editions, one each for grades 1 through 6. The major areas of reading instruction--word skills, vocabulary, study skills, comprehension, and literary forms--are covered as appropriate at each level.

ENRICHMENT READING provides a wide range of activities that target a variety of skills in each instructional area. The program is unique because it helps children expand their skills in playful ways with games, puzzles, riddles, contests, and stories. The high-interest activities are informative and fun to do.

Home involvement is important to any child's success in school. *ENRICHMENT READING* is the ideal vehicle for fostering home involvement. Every lesson provides specific opportunities for children to work with a parent, a family member, an adult, or a friend.

AUTHORS

Peggy Kaye, the author of *ENRICHMENT READING*, is also an author of *ENRICHMENT MATH* and the author of two parent/teacher resource books, *Games for Reading* and *Games for Math*. Currently, Ms. Kaye divides her time between writing books and tutoring students in reading and math. She has also taught for ten years in New York City public and private schools.

WRITERS

Timothy J. Baehr is a writer and editor of instructional materials on the elementary, secondary, and college levels. Mr. Baehr has also authored an award-winning column on bicycling and a resource book for writers of educational materials.

Cynthia Benjamin is a writer of reading instructional materials, television scripts, and original stories. Ms. Benjamin has also tutored students in reading at the New York University Reading Institute.

Russell Ginns is a writer and editor of materials for a children's science and nature magazine. Mr. Ginn's speciality is interactive materials, including games, puzzles, and quizzes.

WHY ENRICHMENT READING?

Enrichment and parental involvement are both crucial to children's success in school, and educators recognize the important role work done at home plays in the educational process. Enrichment activities give children opportunities to practice, apply, and expand their reading skills, while encouraging them to think while they read. *ENRICHMENT READING* offers exactly this kind of opportunity. Each lesson focuses on an important reading skill and involves children in active learning. Each lesson will entertain and delight children.

When children enjoy their lessons and are involved in the activities, they are naturally alert and receptive to learning. They understand more. They remember more. All children enjoy playing games, having contests, and solving puzzles. They like reading interesting stories, amusing stories, jokes, and riddles. Activities such as these get children involved in reading. This is why these kinds of activities form the core of *ENRICHMENT READING*.

Each lesson consists of two parts. Children complete the first part by themselves. The second part is completed together with a family member, an adult, or a friend. *ENRICHMENT READING* activities do not require people at home to teach reading. Instead, the activities involve everyone in enjoyable reading games and interesting language experiences.

Page 65   Your heart beats one hundred thousand times every day!

Page 66   Names will vary.

Page 67   Words and sentences will vary.

Page 68   Words and results will vary.

Page 69 Answers will vary, but should mention something about the pliers.

Page 70 1. 7:50 2. red 3. Bugs and Stan 4. eating dinner 5. Stan was at a birthday party 6. Lou 7. robbing Mrs. Glow 8. Lou

Page 71 Answers will vary.

Page 72 Answers will vary.